Freedom Licence or Liberty?
Engaging with a transforming Ireland

Edited by Harry Bohan

VERITAS

First published 2007 by
Veritas Publications
7/8 Lower Abbey Street
Dublin 1
Ireland
Email publications@veritas.ie
Website www.veritas.ie

ISBN 978 1 84730 028 7

Lines from Emily Dickinson's 'I Dwell in Possibility' taken from *The Poems of Emily Dickinson*, courtesy of Harvard University Press, 1951.

Lines from Seamus Heaney's 'Station Island' taken from *Station Island*, courtesy of Faber & Faber, 1984.

Lines from Louis MacNeice's 'Autumn Journal' taken from Charles Handy's *The Hungry Spirit*, courtesy of Hutchinson, 1997.

A catalogue record for this book is available from the British Library.

Cover by Avid Design
Printed in the Republic of Ireland by Betaprint Ltd, Dublin

Veritas books are printed on paper made from the wood pulp of managed forests. For every tree felled, at least one tree is planted, thereby renewing natural resources.

Contents

Contributors

Fr Harry Bohan, chairman of the Céifin Centre for Values-Led Change, qualified as a sociologist from the University of Wales and is currently Director of Pastoral Planning in the Diocese of Killaloe and parish priest in Sixmilebridge, Co. Clare. In 1998 he founded the Céifin Centre to reflect, debate and direct values-led change in Irish society. He was appointed to the Taskforce on Active Citizenship by An Taoiseach in 2006. Recognised as one of the leading social commentators in Ireland today, Fr Bohan has written extensively on the subjects of Christianity, spirituality and economic development, the importance of the local responding to the global and on understanding change. His publications include *Ireland Green* (1979), *Roots in a Changing Society* (1982), *Hope Begins at Home* (1993) and *Community and the Soul of Ireland: A Conversation with Fr Harry Bohan* with Frank Shouldice (2002). He is editor and contributor to all eight of the publications from previous Céifin conferences and he has broadcast widely on national radio and television. Fr Harry is also well known for his involvment in sport and in Clare hurling in particular.

Frank Daly was appointed Chairman of the Revenue Commissioners in March 2002. He had been a revenue commissioner since 1996 and immediately prior to that had been accountant general of Revenue and head of Strategic and Business Planning. Frank entered Revenue in 1963 when he joined the Customs and Excise Service. He has wide experience of all areas of Revenue including customs, excise, taxes and the international areas. He is a member of the Top Level Appointments Committee, which is the body responsible for selecting top level managers in the Civil Service. Frank was born in Abbeyside, Co. Waterford and educated at Dungarvan C.B.S., University College Dublin and Dublin Institute of Technology.

Mary Davis is Chief Executive Officer of Special Olympics Ireland. Prior to that she served as CEO for the 2003 Special Olympics World Summer Games. Recently appointed by An Taoiseach as Chair of the Taskforce on Active Citizenship, Mary serves on the Council of State and on many committees and boards, including the Irish Sports Council, Campus Stadium Ireland, and is chair of the St Patrick's Festival. She has received honorary doctorates from National University of Ireland, Dublin City University and University of Limerick.

Finola Kennedy is an economist. Educated at the University of Fribourg in Switzerland, UCD and the University of Cambridge, she has been a lecturer in UCD and the Institute of Public Administration. Her principal areas of research are public expenditure and the change in family patterns in the context of economic change. Her book, *Cottage to Creche: Family Change in Ireland* (2001), has been reprinted twice. She was a member of the Review Group on the Constitution and has served or serves on a number of State Boards, including the Housing Finance Agency, ACC Bank and the Railway Procurement Agency.

Alice Leahy is Director of TRUST, which she co-founded in 1975. TRUST is a non-judgemental, befriending, social and health service for people who are homeless. Former Chairman of the Sentence Review Group and recently appointed a member of the Irish Human Rights Commission, Alice is also a writer, commentator, broadcaster and lecturer, promoting understanding of the needs of the outsider in our society to help combat social exclusion. She lectures widely and has directly contributed to public policy as a member of various policy bodies. Alice's most recent book, *With Trust in Place – Writing from the Outside*, which she edited and compiled on the theme of the outsider, has also generated a considerable reaction since its publication in October 2005. In recognition of the work of TRUST Alice was recently awarded an honorary doctorate from UCD and was also named Tipperary Person of the Year in 2004. In addition, Alice has also received a number of other awards over the years and always does so, as she emphasises, on behalf of her colleagues, 'as the work of TRUST is a real team effort'.

Janet Murray is a Director of the Tivoli Institute which is an agency specializing in the provision of training in the field of psychotherapy in Ireland. The Institute provides an extensive community psychotherapy service at its centres in Dublin, Galway and Mayo, and at various centres throughout Ireland in partnership with other organisations. Janet trained in psychoanalytic psychotherapy at Trinity College, Dublin and in London. She is a member of the Irish Forum for Child Psychoanalytic Psychotherapy. She has many years of experience working with psychological and emotional issues in clinical and community settings.

David Quinn is a religious and social affairs commentator. He has been editor of *The Irish Catholic*, a columnist with *The Sunday Times*, and for two and a half years was religious affairs correspondent with *The Irish Independent*. He continues to write weekly columns for *The Irish Independent* and *The Irish Catholic*. David is also a regular contributor to radio and TV current affairs programmes. He is a graduate of Dublin City University.

John Quinn was a senior producer with RTÉ Radio l from 1977 to 2002. His programmes won numerous distinctions, including three Jacobs Awards, and international awards in Japan and New York. His weekly educational magazine *The Open Mind* ran for thirteen years. Born in Ballivor, Co. Meath, he was educated at Patrician College, Ballyfin, Co. Laois and St Patrick's College of Education, Dublin. A former teacher at both primary and post-primary level, he also spent five years as an editor in educational publishing. He has written six novels, five for children, one of which won a Bisto Children's Book of the Year Award, and has edited three best-selling editions of his radio programmes: *A Portrait of the Artist as a Young Girl* (1985), *My Education* (1997) and *The Open Mind Guest Lectures 1989–1998* (1999). Other works include *All Changed* (with Colman Doyle, 2005), a review of how Ireland has changed over the past fifty years, and *Sea of Love, Sea of Loss* (2003), a personal memoir. In February 2003 he was awarded an honorary D.Litt. by the University of Limerick.

Paul Reynolds is a broadcaster and writer and is the crime correspondent for RTÉ. He reports on the activities of major criminals, the criminal justice system, the work of voluntary, local, political and government organisations as well as public policy in this area. He works for all RTÉ outlets – Aertel, RTÉ Online, as well as all radio and television news and current affairs programmes. He was the first person to be appointed to the position of crime correspondent in 1996 following the murders of Detective Garda Jerry McCabe and the journalist Veronica Guerin. He is also the author of two books: *King Scum – The Life and Times of Tony Felloni* (2004), detailing the heroin trade in Ireland and the devastation it causes, and *Sex in the City* (2003), concerning the prostitution racket in this country and those behind it.

Telling My Story

Cian O'Síocháin is a Clareman who came to the world of journalism through a series of story-breaking exercises with the *Limerick Leader*. He continued to freelance in the Limerick area and on the *Evening Echo* news desk. Cian went on to work with

Radio Kerry before a sojourn in Australia. Upon his return to Ireland he furthered his career in media with Newstalk 106 in Dublin, before taking the opportunity to return to his native county as a presenter with Clare FM in 2004.

Salome Mbugua Henry is a native of Kenya and has been living in Ireland for twelve years. She is the founder and national director of AkiDwA (the African Women's Network Ireland). Her background is in social work and gender equality. She has seventeen years experience of working with marginalised groups in Kenya, Uganda and Ireland.

Katherine Chan Mullen graduated as a medical practitioner in the UK in 1976, came to Ireland in 1978, and has worked as a GP in Dublin since 1981. She has been involved in volunteer work for the Chinese community since the 1980s and served as President of the Irish–Chinese Cultural Society for six years in the 1990s. Since 1996 Katherine has been involved with International Orphan Aid, Ireland. Apart from being a volunteer Chinese advisor, she has helped raise money to build a new rehabilitation centre for mentally disabled orphans in Hunan, China and to organise transfer of fourteen orphans to Ireland for medical treatment. Becoming aware of the increasing Chinese community in Ireland, Katherine formed a charity centre to provide free services and information, including a 'hot-line information desk' with bi-lingual Chinese staff. In 2002, the Irish Chinese Information Centre was formally established to continue that work. The centre is also active in establishing and promoting Irish/Chinese cultural exchanges and events such as the Dublin Chinatown Festival.

Adam Rogalinski was born in the town of Poznan in western Poland in 1979. He began his hotel studies at the Academy of Hotel Management in Poznan and later qualified with a degree in Hotel Management in Germany, after which he worked in hotels throughout Europe. In 2001 Adam became aware that

CERT was looking for Polish people to come to Ireland to be trained and work in the hotel industry. He was successful in getting into the CERT bar programme and, over the following five years, has worked in Clare, Kerry and Galway. Adam is now Deputy Manager of Catering in GMIT, Galway. Adam lives in Galway with Kasia, his Polish girlfriend of seven years.

Jose Nilton Vieira de Souza was born in the town of Londrina in Brazil. He arrived in Ireland in 2001 without any English and settled in Gort, Co. Galway. He initially worked for three and a half years in a local hotel. In 2005 Nilton completed the NUIG Diploma in Community Development Practice in Gort and intends to continue to a degree in Community Development. He is very active in several local community development projects in a voluntary capacity and has a particular interest in promoting the integration of Brazilians into Irish society. Nilton is President of the recently established Brazilian Association of Gort. This association was formed to support the local Brazilian community with the everyday difficulties they encounter. Nilton lives with his wife and daughter in Gort where he is self-employed in aspects of construction and interpreting services.

Student Panel

Rachael English is the presenter of *The Constituencies*, a weekly politics programme on RTÉ Radio One. She has worked as a reporter and presenter on most of RTÉ radio's leading current affairs programmes, including *Morning Ireland* and the *News at One*. After six years as presenter of Ireland's most popular drivetime radio programme, *Five Seven Live,* she decided to leave last year. Over the past decade she has covered a huge range of national and international stories for RTÉ from the signing of the Good Friday Agreement to the 2004 Athens Olympics. She is also the co-presenter of RTÉ radio's election results programmes. Rachael received a PPI award (Ireland's national radio awards) for the programme's coverage of the September 11 attacks. During her time as presenter, *Five Seven Live* won all of Ireland's major journalism prizes, including the National Media Award, Justice Media Award and a special award from the National Safety Council for its coverage of road safety.

Sally Ann Flanagan was elected to Tuam Town Council as a candidate for Fine Gael in 2004 at the age of twenty. She was elected as Mayor of Tuam in 2006. Sally Ann works as an administrator in GMIT.

Colm Hamrogue is from Bundoran, Co. Donegal. He holds a degree in Strategic Management and Planning from the Institute of Technology, Sligo. Colm served two years as President of IT Sligo Students' Union before being elected President of the Union of Students of Ireland in May of 2006.

Kieran O'Malley is a native of Ballina, Co. Mayo. He is the USI Western Area Officer. This role involves supporting the full time Student Union Officers in the region. He was elected to the Students' Union in GMIT, acting as Vice President and President in successive years. Kieran is one of the two student hosts of the Céifin National Students' Conference.

In 1999 **Daráine Mulvihill** was struck with a deadly strain of meningitis and septicaemia. Doctors were not hopeful that she would survive and she was given the last rites. Fighting for her life, the doctors were forced to amputate both of her legs below the knee and all of her fingers. Despite these difficulties, Daráine managed to return to her education, graduating from DCU in 2005 with a degree in Communication Studies. In 2006 she completed a postgraduate course in NUI Galway. In 2001, aged eighteen, Daráine received an Irish Person of the Year award. In 2004 she was appointed by President Mary McAleese to be the young person representative on the Irish Council of State.

Foreword

Harry Bohan

The theme of this, our ninth conference, in a way captures what Céifin has being trying to do, namely, engage with a transforming Ireland. The engagement has taken us on a journey, which has hopefully helped many people understand the extraordinary change that is taking place. One of the key messages from this debate has been that change has been so fast, Irish society was and is faced with a whole new phenomenon. Having resolved so many problems in previous years and having become used to doing so, we are now faced with trying to solve problems of which we have no experience, such as: new found and undreamed of affluence; a dismantling of institutions; multiculturalism; fall-out from scandals.

As this New Ireland was being unleashed, the old one was beginning to lose much of its shine. This change is well summed up in a speech given by Vaclav Havel, 'The Need for Transcendence in the Postmodern World', on 4 July 1994 and still very relevant for our time:

> Today many things indicate that we are going through a transitional period when it seems that something is on the way out and something else is painfully being born. It is as if something were crumbling, decaying and exhausting itself, while something else, still indistinct, were arising from the rubble.

There are two notable influences shaping us, both of which represent freedoms we have never before experienced. One is globalisation and the other is growth. Both are relevant to the issues debated in this conference: 'Freedom: Licence or Liberty?'

Globalisation is now central to the emerging nature of society. It can be defined as the free movement of people, ideas, money, trade. The world is our stage and in this way it blurs the distinction between local and global. Shopping in New York, weekends in Paris or Florida are now routine breaks for many people. Global competition and mobility is now introduced into what were, heretofore, largely local allegiances – such as sense of place, neighbours, and community. This is leading to a reworking of tradition. For example, in the world of music a process that began with Sean Ó Riada, continued by others such as Micheál Ó Suilleabháin and complimented in the performing area by groups such as the Chieftains has led to a whole revival of Irish music. It is probably the best example of the local responding to the global. Another example: instead of being part of something because one was born into it, one is now part of something because one selects it. Relationships then are a matter of choice rather than legacy. And this leads to the whole question of trust – earned rather than conferred. This concept of 'active trust' has major implications for relationships.

Growth has taken on a whole new meaning. Economic growth has been central to what and who we have become. The values and language central to this are the values of commerce or market values. The analysis and mechanisms that have brought about this growth is one thing – how to manage it is totally new to us. We have no history to guide us. So herein lies a new challenge. The pace of growth is unprecedented. For example, we are seeing how it is placing ever-increasing stress on the urban infrastructure, making towns and cities increasingly less attractive as places to live and work. As a corollary, rural towns and villages are becoming increasingly attractive to a mobile and globalised population. One of the ironic consequences of this is that as rural areas increase in their attractiveness the 'locals' are finding it increasingly difficult to live and work there. Another consequence of growth is that consumerism is moving us to define ourselves by what we have more than who we are – moving to a state of 'having' from a state of 'being'. A state of having is a condition whereby self-worth is based on having the things central to the consumer age. It would seem to present a fairly major challenge to relationships. Taking into account that our economic transformation is based mainly on technological developments and in particular communications technology we are very definitely presented with major challenges in the area of relationships. The impact the computer has had on society has been unequalled.

One of the very powerful messages from our conferences so far is that despite all the massive changes that are taking place the real struggle is not with the institutions of church or state but with the relentless transfer of power from the family to other influences and agencies. It is not until we come to modern society that we find the isolated nuclear family as it exists today. We have moved in one generation from 'it takes a village to raise a child', to the extended family to the nuclear family to the single parent and other definitions of family.

Who is rearing the next generation? That question was posed after the 1998 conference (*Are We Forgetting Something? Our Society in the New Millennium*). It has been raised often since then. It has presented schools with particular challenges as parents find themselves in an ever-increasing world of 'busy-ness', the aspect of commuting and pressures from the commercial world. At our 2002 conference, *Values and Ethics: Can I Make a Difference?*, in his paper, 'A Framework for a New Reality', John Abbott told us:

> Childhood has become commercialised and, as a nation, we now place a lower priority on teaching our children how to thrive socially, intellectually,

spiritually, than we do on training them to consume which we now do very well. It is as if they were born to buy or to consume what they are fed on TV and Internet.

These are some of the key issues identified in the last nine years. During that same time, Céifin commissioned research into:
- Culture and Ethos of Primary Schools: A study carried out by Noel Canavan, Marino Institute of Education, 2004.
- Family Well Being – What Makes a Difference: A study carried out by Kieran McKeown, Jonathan Pratschke and Trutz Haase, November 2003.
- Well Being and Stress in the Workplace: A study carried out by Mirian Moore, Ph.D., 2002.

All papers have been published and these publications are now valuable sources of interest to a variety of groups and organisations across the country. The debate is also carried into the worlds of education, communities, sport and religion.

As we roll out the papers from the ninth Céifin conference and move towards our tenth anniversary it is time to underline the key messages from the debate of the past decade. Work is now being undertaken on this and we hope to launch it at our conference in November 2007.

The 2006 Conference is divided into four parts:
- Ireland – Where Are We Now?
- Interculturalism: Ireland of the Welcomes?
- Envisioning a New Ireland
- How to Achieve Our Vision

In identifying where we are now:
Finola Kennedy, economist and author of *Cottage to Creche: Family Change in Ireland* (2001) opened the conference with a most enlightening and erudite presentation on the connection

between our economic revolution and our patterns of behaviour. She clearly outlined aspects of the social revolution taking place with the economic revolution and in particular changes in family patterns. Finola clearly outlines where we are now.

Janet Murray followed with an outline of where we are from her own professional experience. Her presentation forces us to confront our society and ourselves and face the notion that 'what we have now is what we want' and in order to progress we need to 'challenge ourselves, to make ourselves and our society stronger and more authentic, so that eventually we and our children can have, not only what we want, but what we truly need as well.'

Paul Reynolds, RTÉ Crime Correspondent, dealt with crime in modern Ireland – how it differs from the past and how it is reported to the wider public.

In dealing with 'Envisioning a New Ireland' four speakers from very different backgrounds emphasised the importance of putting people back into the centre:

Alice Leahy, who has given her life to working with the poorest of the poor, namely, the homeless, reminds us of the importance of treating other people as human beings. 'This is the most basic human right – the right to be treated as a human being and not a statistic,' she says. A faceless bureaucracy doesn't deal well with the most vulnerable of people, which includes the homeless. Their voice is weak.

In suggesting that we have become an acquisitive society rather than an inquisitive one, **John Quinn** emphasised that there are many ways of knowing ourselves and our place in the world. He told us that schooling only accounts for 20 per cent of a young person's life and poses the question, 'what will fill and influence the other 80 per cent?' He went on to suggest ways of doing this.

The chairman of the Revenue Commissioners, **Frank Daly**, welcomed the opportunity to speak on the subject of the links between community and taxation. Having had first-hand experience of dealing with the transformation to a booming economy and a changing workforce he was happy to debate the issue of taxation and a transforming society.

David Quinn questions our perception of freedom. Are we freer in the current climate then we were fifty years ago? It all depends from which vantage point we question it and which type of freedom we refer to.

Finally, **Mary Davis**, CEO of Special Olympics Ireland and chairman of the Taskforce on Active Citizenship, outlined trends in citizen participation in Ireland. Mary's address was rooted in a wealth of knowledge from research and experiences of a broad spectrum of people she dealt with in compiling the governmental report on Active Citizenship.

This conference was different in that the first Céifin National Students' Conference preceded it. That debate was carried into the main conference with a panel of students and young people sharing their ideas on how to achieve our vision. These four young people were: Kieran O'Malley, USI; Sally Ann Flanagan, Mayor of Tuam; Daráine Mulvihill, Graduate DCU and NUIG; Colm Hamrogue, President USI. They all shared their experiences of freedom in a transforming Ireland. We were also delighted to include inputs from a panel of people from different cultures in the 'Telling My Story' session. We are most grateful to these speakers: Salome Mbugua Henry, Kenya; Katherine Chan Mullen, China; Adam Rogalinski, Poland; Nilton Vieira de Souza, Brazil. They offered a valuable insight into Ireland's changing society. The practical experiences of panellists were extremely interesting and enriching. Cian O'Síocháin and Rachael English brought all their interviewing experience to bear on these sessions, thus ensuring a most interesting debate. We are grateful to them, as well as to Anton Savage, for their excellent control of proceedings and contribution to the debate.

We were also delighted to be able to present Alice Leahy with the 2006 Céifin award in recognition of her tireless work on behalf of people in need.

On the organisational side a special word of gratitude is extended to Liam Bluett, Susan Ward and Ciara Griffin from the Céifin office for the many months of planning and preparation. Augmented by a dedicated conference committee, the majority of whom were volunteers, the conference went like clockwork. The support of Bernie, Marguerita and Gloria was, as always, ever present. We are also grateful for the considerable media coverage of the event, as well as the promotional and publicity work carried out on behalf of the conference by Kate Bowe PR.

We gratefully acknowledge the support of all our sponsors. To them, the management and staff of the West County Hotel, Ennis, and to everyone who attended as delegates and who brought so much to the proceedings, we say 'thanks'.

Fr Harry Bohan
March 2007

Ireland: Where are we now?

The Best of Times, the Worst of Times

Finola Kennedy

Introduction

It is great to be in Ennis, a town where history has been made and continues to be made. Strolling through the town this morning, I was reminded of Daniel O'Connell's glorious election to Westminster. I wonder how this giant of Irish history would view Ennis today. How would he view Ireland today? I hope that he would be pleased. Seán Ó Faoláin called his biography of O'Connell *King of the Beggars*. O'Connell would surely rejoice in the prosperity of the people. O'Connell stood for freedom and so touches the central theme of this conference. It is a privilege to be invited to address the ninth Céifin conference and I would like to thank Fr Harry Bohan for his invitation. It is a bonus to be the first speaker as in a short while I can sit back and enjoy the excellent line-up, including a group of 'new Irish' and a group of third-level students and recent graduates.

For many people in Ireland today these are the best of times; for some these are the worst of times. For many, contemporary Ireland is an Aladdin's Cave of wealth and opportunity, attracting hundreds of thousands of immigrants. Immigration flows provide a mirror image of another Ireland, when Irish emigrants were attracted to foreign lands hoping to find streets paved with gold, far from the poverty of their rural villages and urban tenements. Today, one in ten of the population of 4.2 million is an immigrant.

It is thrilling to be alive in Ireland at a time of full employment. For too long our study of economics focused bleakly on unemployment. While a successful economy can not be taken for granted, and continued success requires continued endeavour as well as some good luck, it is now claimed with some justification that our problems are those of a successful economy. As the economy has flourished there is evidence that more remains to be done by both government and governed, leaders and citizens, to apply the fruits of prosperity to build an inclusive and caring community where each child is all our children. For in the words of an African saying, made famous by Hillary Clinton in her book of that title, 'it takes a village to raise a child'. In a nutshell, material progress has been magnificent; moral development in the sense of discerning rights and wrongs as well as distinguishing right from wrong remains a challenge. Today, possibly as we speak, someone's child is committing suicide, someone's child is being killed on the roads, and this week someone's child will be murdered. These are what the chill statistics tell us. Of what use is it to these people and their families that GNP is growing by more than 5 per cent per year?

The organisers of this conference have selected an important but complex theme. Freedom has many facets. I will look at two – the use of freedom for socio-economic purposes and the use of freedom in the sphere of personal relationships – in the context of where we are now.

Socio-Economic Freedom

As this year is the ninetieth anniversary of the Rising, it occurred to me to start by asking what was Pearse's vision of where we might be now. In an article published in *Spark* in April 1916 entitled 'The Heart's Desire', Pearse said that in a free Ireland its legislators would be honest and capable and its education system would help every man and woman to become a perfect citizen. There would be work for every man and woman and the population would expand to twenty million in a century.[1]

This year is also the eightieth anniversary of the foundation of Fianna Fáil. Of the approximately eighty-five years of self-government, Fianna Fáil has held power for two-thirds of the time, approximately fifty-five years. Because of its dominance it is worth looking at where Fianna Fáil hoped us to be now. Fianna Fáil's vision was set out in the seven aims of its Constitution.[2] These included the unity and independence of Ireland as a Republic, the restoration of the Irish language, the making of Ireland as far as possible economically self-contained and self-sufficient, and the carrying out of the Democratic Programme of the First Dáil. The Democratic Programme had itself placed the care of children as 'the first duty of the Republic'.

If one were to benchmark achievement against these goals, it is fairly obvious that the score would be low. Rather we know that Ireland has achieved significant material success by deliberately abandoning many, if not all, of those goals. This is the case, for example, in regard to economic self-sufficiency, a goal pursued at a punishing cost in the 1930s, but which was abandoned in the late 1950s. The nation moves on. In his speech at the opening of the 1916 Exhibition at the National Museum at Collins's Barracks on 9 April 2006, the Taoiseach said: 'The decision to join the European Union was the moment when a confident and hopeful Ireland left behind what had become the dated and sterile ideology of "ourselves alone".'

Nowhere has 'Ourselves Alone' (Sinn Féin) become so obviously outdated as with the inflow of immigrants on whom we rely to keep the economy on the march. Substantial immigration has increased the multiculturalism of society. Today's Ireland includes not only faiths represented by church, synagogue and mosque but a variety of Eastern, African and other belief systems. At the same time all the religions compete with secularism. We are part of a global economy in which the twelve stars of Europe tell as much about who we are as the green, white and orange. Irish economic policy is moulded in Brussels and monetary policy is forged in Frankfurt. It was in the context of the European and global economy that the Celtic Tiger leaped onto the scene.

Economic development and social change go hand in hand. Roy Foster observes that over the past thirty years, 'sexual Puritanism, narrow nationalism and economic protectionism have been jettisoned with unholy speed'.[3] This has happened in the world of the 'Pope's Children'.[4] I may not be one of the 'Pope's Children' but I am grounded in their reality, partly as a result of being the mother of a few of those children and there is much to welcome in the success and freedom of that generation.

Central to David McWilliams's vibrant book is the emergence in the 1990s of a new class of Irish people who combine features of Hibernian and Cosmopolitan. In his luminous book, *The Transformation of Ireland 1900-2000*,[5] Diarmaid Ferriter shows that class, often thought not to be applicable to Irish history, is clearly illustrated by a catalogue of rejected persons: 'migrants, orphans and unmarried mothers'. So let's not idealise an imagined Paradise Lost – a paradise which did not in fact exist but included the darker aspects of Irish life depicted by historians, including Joe Lee and Diarmaid Ferriter, and writers including John McGahern and Tom Murphy, and researchers Mary Raftery and Eoin O'Sullivan. At the other end of the scale a large class of holders of 'new wealth' has emerged. Overall this wealth must be welcomed, as must the generosity of many of the holders of this wealth. Yet if one were to look for an ironic contemporary symbol of modern Ireland, it could perhaps be found in the collecting by a few rich businessmen of the paintings of possibly the greatest Irish painter of the twentieth century – Jack Yeats. For Yeats' paintings are filled with travellers and tinkers and others relegated to the margins. Only in paintings have the travellers and tinkers infiltrated the drawing rooms of the rich. In a way, everything changes, yet nothing changes. In the current exhibition *A Time and a Place* in the

National Gallery, there is a magnificent painting of 'Market Day, Ennis', circa 1825. In the painting, Turner de Lond highlights the class contrast between the ladies and the country women. The role of the latter is depicted as close to beasts of burden.

Despite the move from narrow nationalism via the abandonment of Articles 2 and 3 of the Constitution, despite greater economic freedom and freedom to reject sexual puritanism, despite Irish victory in the Cheltenham Gold Cup, the Grand National and the Triple Crown, despite the wonderful success of the Ryder Cup, there is a sense of malaise. Brendan Gleeson's outburst on the *Late Late Show* earlier this year about hospital trolleys in the midst of plenty could perhaps be taken as a metaphor of the malaise. John Boorman's film, *The Tiger's Tail*, in which Gleeson stars, highlights this issue in the context of contemporary Ireland. Such problems are not new; what is new is the fact that greatly increased wealth in Ireland has led to the expectation that such problems should be solved – that the resources are available to do the job, but some fault line in the system, perhaps lack of political will, has blocked resolution. There are signs that the national conscience has been stirred.

To grow means simply to increase in size. With growth we have lost our small national schools, our local garda stations, our small post offices and neighbourhood letter boxes. Postal collections and deliveries are reduced. Sole practice GPs are vanishing. House calls by GPs are virtually extinct. The days of small hospitals are numbered. Children are bussed to bigger and more distant schools. All of this growth in the size of service delivery units is done in the name of efficiency. Certainly there is justification for rationalisation but hardly for all the 'rationalisation' of services, especially when reduction in services is accompanied by an increase in bureaucracy. Bureaucracy itself, often riding on the back of some worthy and expensive consultancy report, can then itself become the problem. And a new phenomenon has emerged with the growth of bureaucracy – the replacement of human beings at the end of phone lines with 'pre-recorded menus' interspersed with 'tunes'. Thus, for example, if one wants to make a complaint to Eircom that one's phone is out of action for reasons other than those on the 'menu', one is likely to remain hungry. It is even difficult to get through to a human being in the Revenue Commissioners, although I know they exist there in large numbers!

Growth on an international scale has also been associated with misuse of resources. The environmental 'plunder of the planet' has indeed become an 'inconvenient truth' and the Green Agenda now begins to make economic sense. More people are living alone today than ever before, that is, living outside the context of any immediate household relationship. When the state was founded very few persons lived alone; now more than one in five lives alone. In the 1920s less than one in twenty persons over 65 lived alone; now more than one-quarter lives alone. In 2004, over one in three women and just one in four men over 65 years lived alone. Some undefined feelings are in circulation which seem to suggest that the economic prizes have been won at a wounding cost.

Freedom in Personal Relationships

The ebb and flow of personal relationships is not independent from the socio-economic currents. In some important respects those currents have been flowing in opposite directions. Today when the role of state economic enterprise has been removed or reduced mainly due to privatisation, the role of the state in providing 'home' services through the care of children and the elderly has never been more extensive. A curious shift is taking place: as the economy moves more in the direction of private enterprise and the market, more Boston than Berlin, many traditional functions of the home are shifting towards the state. The move out of the home to service the economy is having the effect of increasing demands on the state for services previously provided on a voluntary basis at home. At a time when the price of houses is the hottest topic in town, it is ironic that houses have never been more empty of human life and activity for longer periods of the day.

At the same time it would be false to make distinctions that are too rigid. Just as 'private enterprise' is supported by a plethora of grants and tax breaks, so too private individuals are helped in their caring functions by supports which include child benefit and carer's allowance. The state also assists the private provision of, for example, hospitals and crèches, via major tax breaks. The provision of crèches and homes for the elderly are big business today.

Accompanying the shift towards the provision by the state of services formerly provided by the people in their own homes, or frequently by various religious orders and voluntary groups, there has been a shift in policy towards the prioritisation of market work over work in homes. The moves towards the individualisation of the tax system introduced in Budget 2000 provided incentives for labour force, as distinct from household, work. Childcare is an issue for bosses as well as babies and their parents.

And now to sexual matters. For most people in Ireland, until the final quarter of the twentieth century it was probably the case that marriage was the essential context for sexual relations. Access to contraception broke that link. Births outside marriage accounted for one-third of births in 2005, exceeding half of all births in Limerick city. Girls under the age of consent (seventeen years) gave birth to 224 babies in 2005. Some 42 births were to girls younger than sixteen and of those two girls had each previously had a child. In 2006 one seventeen-year-old gave birth to her fourth child. Many surveys show the increase in sexual activity among young people. This has been accompanied by an increase in sexually transmitted infections. The spread of these infections has been firmly linked to alcohol abuse by expert, Dr Derek Freedman.[6]

Following the introduction of divorce which is now at the level of one in six marriages, low by the standards of other developed countries, marriage enters the category of agreements which may be terminated on grounds other than death, a feature of cohabitation and partnerships. With divorce, the dividing line between marriage and cohabitation is no longer so clear cut, and the definition of 'family' becomes more complex. The growth in cohabitation in Ireland has been marked, with close to 80,000 family units, or over 8 per cent of all family units, now based on cohabitation.

The reality of divorce and of cohabitation has been widely recognised and accepted. Speaking at a conference in Sussex in July 2005, the Catholic Archbishop of Dublin, Dr Diarmaid Martin, said:

> Many young people have acclimatised themselves to the values of contemporary society. Many do not wish to formally marry. Many if not most will live together for shorter or longer periods before they finally get married. Divorce is not desired but most of our Christian believer[s] would consider it not just a necessary evil but perhaps even a valuable institution. It is interesting that many of those young people who set out on such a path develop into excellent spouses and parents, learning marital and parental abilities you might say from nature itself rather than through any formal catechesis on the part of the Church.[7]

This statement reflects the realities of life, as distinct from a statement of theory. Arensberg and Kimball, the American sociologists who authored a classic study of the Irish family in the 1930s with field work based here in Co. Clare, argued that everything a man did or was in rural Ireland in the 1930s could be referred to his blood or what was colourfully called, in the words of a rural TD, the 'the stud book'. Today, conflict is more likely to centre on the difficulties in reconciling lifestyle freedom with home and work responsibilities even if the maintenance of property according to the 'stud book' may never go away entirely.

Looking Ahead

In his satirical work of genius, *The Midnight Court,* Clareman Brian Merriman suggested that sexual pleasures should be left to nature, unfettered by the restrictions of marriage and the Church:

> Down with marriage! Tis out of date,
> It exhausts the stock and cripples the state.
> The priest has failed with whip and blinker,
> Now give a chance to Tom the tinker,
> And mix and mash in nature's can
> The tinker and the gentleman;
> Let lovers in every lane extended,
> Follow their whim as God intended,
> And in their pleasure bring to birth
> The morning glory of the earth.[8]

Merriman was mourning the *emergence* of Catholic puritanism. While a contemporary Merriman would hardly urge the return of the 'whip and blinker', he might utter a few warnings about the seemingly unstoppable rise of sales of the 'morning-after' pill. Sexual activity requires some minimum of social control to avoid, *inter alia*, the spread of disease. Given that the age of consent for sexual relations both heterosexual and homosexual is seventeen years, and given the fact that surveys have shown considerable underage sexual activity and many births to mothers below the age of consent, should policy try to limit underage sex or is the realistic thing to reduce the age of consent to sixteen years as it was from 1885 to 1935? This is an important question.

Who will care for the children and for the elderly? These are other key questions and how they are addressed reflects the relative priority which we attach to paid work and to family life in its widest sense. What is the relative respect which society really accords to the largely voluntary work within the household, as distinct from paid work in the workplace? With more children born outside marriage, how can a child best have access to both parents? For the 20,000 children born outside marriage each year, there is no legal right at birth to know who their father is, or to have contact with their father. Notwithstanding the position in Irish law, the UN Convention on the Rights of the Child, which was ratified by the Irish Government in 1992, states that every child has a right to knowledge of both parents and, as far as possible, to be cared for by both parents. Karl Marx once told his daughter, Jenny, 'We can forgive Christianity much because it taught us the worship of the child'.[9] How much do we really value and respect children? At the other end of the age spectrum how much do we really value the elderly – the children grown old? The number and proportion of elderly people in the population is set to grow rapidly. According to Minister Brennan, 900,000 future pensioners have either no pension provision or inadequate provision. Nursing home scandals, references to 'bed blockers' and 'warehousing' the elderly are chilling. Christianity does not just involve a 'tip-toeing' back to the churches. That could be the easier part. It demands the service of one's fellow human being of all creeds and none, for as the great French writer, Charles Péguy, wrote, 'we can not go to God alone'.

In a fundamental way, in the sense of creating a social environment, embedded in a safe and secure physical environment, in which it is possible for lives to be lived and for people to die within a network of relationships which are intimate enough to be human, we need to create a 'social village' with some of the features of the old village. I am not talking about maidens at the crossroads or about jiving at the crossroads but rather about a society in which both government and governed share a common purpose and participation in that enterprise is facilitated at *local level*. Legislators legislate on our behalf and government should provide a fair tax system in which everyone pays a decent amount in relation to their income and wealth and where the tax cheat is punished and the tax exile becomes the self-selected outcast – the truly marginal man. Did those who left Ireland when the potato failed dream that other Irishmen would leave because they did not wish to share the abundant fruits of their success by paying tax?

At the core of the social network is the family unit, however broadly or narrowly defined. From that intimate nucleus grows true citizenship, for in the words of Edmund Burke, 'to love the little platoon we belong to is the germ of all public affection'. If opportunity and responsibility are reflected in how we design our service provision and taxation system, then community will develop. A nation's budget is more than a book-keeping exercise. It is a litmus test of a nation's values.

Modern technology opens a world of opportunity. The Internet can be used to make and retain contacts. Local radio is of great value in forming and strengthening communities and has potential for further development. Ennis has been a pioneer in this area. Voluntary activity as a facet of active citizenship is available to all who are able and who wish to participate. If everyone who is able to do so were to join one of the multitude of voluntary organisations which exist in the country and give a minimum of two hours per week in some work of service, the country and its citizens would be transformed. If no organisation appeals directly to you, then start your own. This is precisely what one young woman, fourteen-year-old Anita McCluskey, whose sister Claire was killed in the Navan bus crash, did when she set up the Seedlings Group to support the bereaved. Think of how a world wide organisation like Alcoholics Anonymous was founded and take courage. There is a time in our lives when most of us are fit and able to do some volunteering; let's not delay. The establishment of the Taskforce on Active Citizenship is just one step in the right direction.

At the start I quoted from Pearse's ideal that education would lead every man and woman into perfect citizenship. That challenge remains. To take up that challenge we need inspirational leadership which will help to carve out pathways to citizenship and to lead the people on those pathways. Leaders of the State and of the Churches must be 'honest and capable'; they must be brave; they must take risks and remember that we do not live by bread alone.

The European Values Study shows that freedom, understood as personal autonomy, is the most important value for modern Europeans. Timothy Radcliffe, the Dominican, who once famously remarked that everything in Catholicism was either forbidden or compulsory, suggests that freedom begins when people grasp the choices they may make, even if extremely limited. Thus at Auschwitz, above which portal was inscribed in iron 'Arbeit Macht Frei' (Through Labour – Freedom),[10] a prisoner said to his fellow prisoner, Primo Levi:

> We are slaves, deprived of every right, exposed to every insult, condemned to certain death, but we still possess one power, and we must defend it with all our strength for it is the last – the power to refuse our consent.[11]

Freedom is, then, something precious, and its exercise is a responsibility. There is a huge difference between the condition of freedom and that of accepting no responsibility to anyone. Important as political leadership undoubtedly is, we are where we are, less perhaps, as a result of the visions of dead political leaders, 'though those dead men are loitering there to stir the boiling pot', and more as a result of consent given and withheld by our dead parents and grandparents. The Proclamation of 1916 began with the words, 'In ainm Dé agus in ainm na nglún d'imig romhainn': In the name of God and of the dead generations. So let us remember those dead, not alone those who died but those who chose to live for their ideals. The future will be shaped by our own personal choices, within the range of options available to us, perhaps more than we realise.

Notes

1 Ruth Dudley Edwards, *Patrick Pearse: The Triumph of Failure*, London: Gollancz, 1977, p. 338.
2 The seven aims of the Fianna Fáil Constitution are:
   • To secure the Unity and Independence of Ireland as a Republic.
   • To restore the Irish language as the spoken language of the people and to develop a distinctive national life in accordance with Irish traditions and ideals.
   • To make the resources and wealth of Ireland subservient to the needs and welfare of all the people of Ireland.
   • To make Ireland, as far as possible, economically self-contained and self-sufficient.
   • To establish as many families as practicable on the land.
   • By suitable distribution of power to promote the ruralisation of industries essential to the lives of the people as opposed to their concentration in cities.
   • To carry out the Democratic Programme of the First Dáil.
3 In his review of Diarmaid Ferriter's book, *The Transformation of Ireland 1900–2000, Guardian*, 13 November 2004.
4 David McWilliams, *The Pope's Children, Ireland's New Elite*, Dublin: Gill & Macmillan, 2005.
5 London: Profile Books Ltd., 2004.
6 *Pat Kenny Show*, RTÉ Radio 1, 20 September 2006.
7 Diarmuid Martin, 'Gaudium et spes: The Unaddressed Issues', Sussex, 6 July 2005.
8 Brian Merriman, *The Midnight Court*, trans. by Frank O'Connor, Dublin: O'Brien Press, 1989.
9 Francis Wheen, *Karl Marx: A Life*, New York: W.W. Norton & Company, 2000, p. 215.
10 Niall Ferguson, *The War of the World*, London: Allen Lane, 2006, p. 220.
11 Timothy Radcliffe, *What is the Point of Being a Christian?*, London: Burns & Oates, 2005, p. 36.

What We Have is What We Want

Applying the Values of Psychotherapy to our Current Social Dilemmas

Janet Murray

Most people here today will share a concern about the downsides of the current era of prosperity in Ireland. These downsides are known to include a loss of community, the dominance of consumerism, the loss of a sense of meaning for individuals and groups and so on. There are many views on why this should be so. There is an entire discourse based on sociology which seeks to put forward reasons and rationales. Other arguments and discourses on these themes are perhaps more political and philosophical. My work as a psychotherapist brings me into contact with a variety of human problems and issues. The vantage point of the clinician naturally allows me to get inside some of the labels and clichés and relate to the real unique individual. Nothing is ever as it seems and few of you will be surprised to hear that. Many people who present for psychotherapy report an unwillingness or incapacity in our culture to listen with insight and awareness. We like people to be normal. That's all we want to know about.

No doubt some people here suspect that psychotherapy is part of the problem and not useful in pointing towards solutions. For some, psychotherapy reinforces the individualistic strain in our culture which appears to be now to the fore. Psychotherapy can be attacked by some as a form of privatisation, an indulgence for the rich and famous, even an outright rejection of communitarian values. For others, the very practice of psychology in any form is inherently suspicious and potentially invasive. Of course you must know now that I am analysing all of you as I stand here, reading your very thoughts and quietly shaking my head, knowingly but despairingly!

Instead of defending psychotherapy or suggesting that it is a panacea for all our ills I would like instead to use some of the core ideas from psychotherapy outside of their usual context in the therapy room and apply them to some of our social dilemmas. While needing to be provocative and challenging there is always the danger that any form of psychological probing will give rise to even greater resistance and denial than already exists. This conference has always been about Irish society and the evolving Irish culture. I believe it is important in examining that evolving culture from a psychological point of view to be empathic and not judgemental, constructive and not condemnatory, insightful and action oriented rather than dogmatic and stultifying. The culture is not some vague concept or smart excuse for an Arts Council grant but is something here and now. It is about me and it is about you.

We can always defend ourselves against emotional disturbance or discomfort by standing apart and saying, 'it's them, not me'. We can also defend by sheer denial saying, 'it's not happening', or 'it might be happening but I don't see it'. Some of us defend by manic activity, by displacing all our energies and responses into manic busy-ness. It is also important for some to be important. Arguably we have far more people around concerned with being important than we ever had before. Obsessive importance is a defence too. In prosperity we tend to grow more people with an important and narcissitic sense of destiny. Sometimes what we mean, psychologically, when we talk about concepts like community is a zone where there are fewer defences of this type, and less need for them and more emotional contact between people than might otherwise be the case. If we lack a sense of community perhaps we have a preference for the safety and apparent certainty of defences instead.

Despite all these defences and other psychological strategies there is evidence in our culture of deep unease. To take the most glaring and obvious example, most of you will know that we have the highest per capita consumption of alcohol of almost any advanced country. You may already be weary and despairing of this example. Weariness and despair can sometimes be defences against being touched at a deeper level. To place the matter in context we have three times the per capita consumption of the Germans. We also have a clearly identified pattern of destructive binge drinking on a scale unmatched anywhere. In addition, some of you will be aware of an international debate that has gone on for many years among psychologists and psychiatrists about the Irish as an ethnic group and our over-representation in statistics on admissions to mental health facilities world wide. Our migrant's rates of depression, schizophrenia, addiction, anxiety disorders etc. have been recorded as far higher than the indigenous population and cannot be explained by the fact of migration alone. Other migrant ethnic groups such as the Afro-Caribbeann group have had nothing like the same rate of admissions as the Irish. Not many of us relish having to face up to figures such as these. We want to project a positive self-image and don't want to return to the bad old days of feeling inferior to the colonial power. That is an understandable defence.

We know that in the past we had what we might call poverty drinking. That served as an explanation of sorts. Excessive drinking and poverty were assumed to be connected. Now it seems we have 'affluent drinking'. Excessive drinking and affluence are assumed to be connected. The excuses are wearing thin. The binging is increasing, not decreasing, it is worse this year than it was last year. It is not about opening hours or advertising. It will not change because we enact more laws to discourage it. It is about ourselves and only we can change it. It is about our relationship with ourselves. It is about our mental health. Binge drinking is not the celebration it appears but has always been a sign of deep unhappiness. Binge drinking on our scale and at our pace is not a party. Quite the contrary, it is more like a wake, and our society is potentially the corpse. What would happen if this outlet were to be taken away? What is it that we can do, think and say during our binges that we cannot do in our sober state? What unnamed inner frustration or pain does the binging relieve? Is this destructive behaviour a sign that at a deep level we don't value ourselves? We still don't know why we drink so much. Perhaps we don't as a nation like to question why. That reluctance to ask is a defence.

What is indeed most striking is our collective refusal to explore the real psychological roots of this long-standing distressed and distressing behaviour. We display a general lack of psychological curiousity about it. Perhaps we are resigned or perhaps we really don't want to know. What we have is what we want. Who wants to understand the psychology of it? That would spoil the grim fun.

Indeed, to think and speculate in psychological terms at all is regarded in our culture with suspicion, as a kind of letting the side down, a damp squib. The negative stigma we generate in relation to mental health issues and those afflicted by them is matched only by our refusal to think psychologically about social and personal issues. To give a recent example, an expert group on mental health in Ireland, established by the Minister for Health and Children, Mary Harney, and comprised of leading psychiatrists, psychologists, psychotherapists and others, issued its report in January 2006 after two years of deliberation and extensive consultation. A psychotherapist colleague of mine at the Tivoli Institute was a member of the group. Its report, appropriately entitled 'A Vision for Change', contains much that is thought provoking and stimulating but was given derisory coverage in the newspapers and other media. In *The Irish Times* it got three column inches on page seven for just one day. Mental health issues affect one in four of the population. It is very likely that as an ethnic group we are significantly more affected than other ethnic groups. So we give it three column inches on page seven. If it had been a 'vision for change' for the Irish Stock Exchange or the Irish Race Horse industry, I guarantee it would have made the front page with prominent headlines and on more than one day. This is what we want to be the case. To be curious about psychological issues is too threatening. It seems safer to collude in a collective stigma. That too is a defence.

Let's ask some more awkward questions. If community values of old were so important and dear to us then why have so many of us colluded in their near abandonment? How have we done this on so many levels? Is it possible that little real or authentic community ever existed, that there was little emotional contact taking place? Might this explain how quickly the appearance of community was abandoned? Or was it that instead of authentic communication and caring between people we had merely a sense of solidarity in poverty, an interdependence that rarely went further than functional cooperation? If the elderly were ever valued and revered and included in our communities as we tell ourselves they were, then why have we now shunted them to one side so quickly and treat them as irrelevant to our collective pursuits? The notion of family has always been held up as an ideal, as an answer to all manner of social problems. Yet there was always so much going on in families that did not fit with this idealisation. The family is a complex entity. If we can be nurtured in families we can also be destroyed in families. All of us here know this. The surface appearance and what is supposed to happen is very different to what really transpires. The truth about family is held by all of us as private knowledge which finds little space in the public sphere. Our culture does not permit the more complex reading of family and its potential toxicity as well as potential strengths. Why is this so? Are we afraid of the necessary depression that such public disillusionment around family might bring? Have we no faith that after disillusionment we might find more solid ground for ourselves and our culture?

Another question. Structures are important. Living a long way from the workplace and having to commute long hours is not necessarily something the individual can manage long term and has a huge impact on the quality of life and on mental health. But apparently immoveable structures and strictures in the world can mask the degree to which we collude with the forces that shape us. For example, Dublin is now held up internationally as an instance of how not to plan a city. It is celebrated internationally as a planning fiasco. A city with a relatively small population manages to sprawl over an area greater than Los Angeles. Commuting dominates and damages so many lives. It makes the development of community almost impossible. Why did we let this happen despite the many warnings over so many years? It is not all down to politicians taking bribes. Don't we value ourselves enough to protest effectively? It is often said that we are more individualistic nowadays, but are we? If a large group are following a similar path in the direction of corporate profit at the expense of other values or even in the direction of disastrous city planning, how can we say, in any meaningful sense, that they are individualistic? Surely it is more true to say that we live in a deeply conformist time where little real individuality is to be found. Conformism, which is a defence, is now on a scale and at a depth that it has become difficult to see it for what it is. Consumerism on the scale now evident here is about conforming and conformism is always rooted in deep anxiety. Why are we so afraid to appear different, to break with the herd? What is this anxiety about? Is it the old existential anxiety about who I am and why I'm here which is denied and avoided by means of addictions or defences? Or is it something else? Is it about our fear of limits and boundaries, the fact that we die and others around us die, the fact that we can't merge with someone else to avoid the pain of life however much we might want to? Do we lack real confidence to be ourselves and for that to be enough? Does that explain our conformity?

Certainly in the past we afflicted ourselves with impossible ideals and impossible loyalties resulting in the splitting of the psyche between light and dark, good and bad, sober and drunk, outwardly conformist and inwardly rebellious. Is this splitting still going on in us only in a more disguised form? Do we find it difficult to be whole people in the world rather than split people? Are we afraid we might become too boring to ourselves if we became whole? Are we afraid to be criticised, to have to stand alone without defences, just as we are? Hand-wringing and blaming always seems preferable to any kind of accurate self-reflection, to the hard work of seeing our part in how things are. It is only when we give up our blaming of others, of circumstances, of fate or even of God and take responsibility for how we are now and what we have created, that we make progress. What we have is what we want. It must be the case. There is nobody to blame. It is not easy to stop blaming. It is not easy to see our part in things as they are. But that is the only way that personal change or any real change takes place.

Our apparent lack of psychological capacity leaves us ill-equipped to help our young people, to support them with psychological insight and awareness. We know that young men in their late teens and twenties are committing suicide at an increasing rate. In each case there are stages on the way to such tragic acts. These stages are internal, not usually externalised. Young men need us to be attuned to this, not hiding in our defences or our complacency. It is well known that young girls and young women in the 14–21 age group are increasingly prone to self-starvation on the one hand and obesity on the other. These extremes are very striking and, especially with self-starvation, quite alarming. Eating disorders in this age group are fast becoming the norm, not the exception. The regression to a pre-pubescent appearance among many young women suggests a deep unease with the progression towards womanhood. Young women in this age group are in a group which is desired. Our collective culture projects onto them in terms of expectation, longing, frustration, sexual and otherwise. They are set up as 'the models', metaphorically and sometimes in reality. Is full-bodied womanhood too difficult a step for them to take and, if so, why? Surely young women need all of us to be attuned to these pressures, to be able to interpret accurately and empathically what might be happening at a deeper level.

What is clearly needed now is a new psychological sophistication grounded in psychological curiousity and characterised by a willingness to ask the hard and searching questions. We have to be prepared to enter the zone of useful but still perhaps frightening confusion before we discover what is solid and what is ephemeral. We have to challenge our defences and avoidances, to subject our comfortable beliefs and defensive habits to scrutiny, not in order to weaken ourselves but to make ourselves and our society stronger and more authentic so that eventually we and our children can have, not only what we want, but what we truly need.

Crime in Ireland

Paul Reynolds

I have held the position of Crime Correspondent for RTÉ for the past ten years. RTÉ is the only twenty-four hour news service in the country. I work for radio, television, online and Aertel, and my deadline is the next news bulletin which is usually at the top of the hour. I work for all radio news bulletins and programmes – such as *Morning Ireland*, the *News at One* and the *This Week* programme, as well as radio current affairs programmes like *The Pat Kenny Show*, *The Gerry Ryan Show* and *Drivetime* with Mary Wilson. I also work for all television news and current affairs programmes – the *One*, *Six-One*, *Nine* news on RTÉ 1 and *Late News* on RTÉ 2, as well as *Primetime*. I report on all aspects of crime and the criminal justice system, government and opposition policy, the work of the courts, the Gardaí, the legal profession and the prison service. Due to the nature of broadcasting, the television and radio reports I produce for the news bulletins are usually between forty seconds and two and a half minutes long. However, the news and current affairs programmes usually allow more time for greater analysis and explanation.

I have also written two books, which have allowed me to further research and examine specific areas of crime in Ireland today. *Sex in the City* (2003) is about the prostitution industry and argues that, far from it being a harmless profession rooted in freedom of choice, it is a seedy, sinister and seriously damaging criminal enterprise. *King Scum – The Life and Times of Tony*

Felloni (2004) is about the drugs trade, specifically the heroin business, told through the life of one man and his family.

The reality is that a large proportion of the incidents I report on happen late at night or in the early hours of the morning – violent attacks, shootings, Garda raids, murders. Most of my time is spent reporting on or trying to analyse, assess or explain some of the most awful, tragic and horrific events that can possibly occur in people's lives. Tragically and all too often, it is not people's lives but people's deaths that I have to report on.

Impact of Media Reporting/Fear of Crime

Crime is an issue of major public interest. It is, therefore, covered extensively in the media. In the tabloid media in particular it dominates and dictates the news agenda along with entertainment and celebrity, sport, sex, scandal and health – most notably health scares or medical phenomena.

Crime is an area which both appals and fascinates because it directly or indirectly affects us all. Anybody who has not been a victim of crime knows someone who has been a victim at some level. Many of us make our living from crime, not just reporters and robbers, but also Gardaí, lawyers, prison officers – even the Minister for Justice. There is no doubt that crime hits us all in our pockets because through our taxes we pay for the police service. An increase in certain types of crime will cost us more. A rise in shoplifting will mean prices in the shops go up; a rise in burglary or car crime means an increase in the insurance premiums we pay.

Many people find the other important issues such as politics, economics or religious affairs boring. There is no doubt that who governs us, how much we have to live on and whether or not there is a God are hugely important, but very often these issues are complicated, abstract and difficult to understand. Crime, however, is a lot more simple and direct. Crime stories directly impact on people's lives in a way that people can understand very quickly. They also produce an immediate visceral reaction – sympathy, empathy, smugness, and/or snobbery, a feeling or belief that this could never happen to me or that the victim had it coming. Crime stories grab people's attention and sell newspapers. Since the death of Veronica Guerin in 1996 there has been a dramatic increase in crime reporting and reporters. It is not just RTÉ; every national newspaper has at least one reporter specialising in crime. There is, therefore, a lot of crime news around, a lot of hype and sensation, fantasy as well as fact.

The media will argue that there is more reporting because there is a greater interest and demand from the public in crime stories. But along with this interest comes also the element of fear. With all this new and detailed knowledge of crime – particularly violent crime and the criminal underworld – there is now an element of fear of crime in the community. Is the increase in crime reporting contributing to this fear?

Ironically, the fact is that those least likely to be victims of crime are those likely to be most afraid, i.e. the elderly. And those most likely to be victims are least afraid, i.e. young men in their teens and twenties. So while old people remain hidden and frightened in their homes, young people pay no care and are out and about on the so-called mean streets. And older people – even though they are most afraid – still can't get enough of what scares them.

In spite of what the journalists and the politicians – usually the opposition politicians – say, this fear of crime is not really justified by the statistics. The fact is that statistically we in Ireland still have a relatively low crime rate. There might be fifty murders a year here; there can be fifty a night in New York or Johannesburg. So should we stop reporting serious crime such as murder here because there is the danger that we are frightening people to death? Clearly I don't believe so. If we did I'd be out of a job! But the fact is that we in Ireland still have a different attitude to serious crime, in particular murder, than the public or the media do in, say, Britain or the US. Murder is the most serious crime that can be committed. The media in other countries may not report all murders but we in RTÉ and most of the Irish media do. Why? For my own and RTÉ's part, and I suspect it is the same for other media here, it is because we believe human life is sacred. The taking of human life is inherently wrong and shocking and we as a media organisation have a responsibility to recognise, report and highlight that. The day we walk away, downgrade or fail to report these offences, no matter how common or uncommon they become, is the day we lose part of our value system, part of our sense of moral outrage, part of our humanity.

The Reality of Crime Today

There has been an increase in the number of murders and incidents of manslaughter in the past ten years, but it has been a gradual increase. The figures for homicides show that in 1995 there were 51 homicides; last year there were 58. Over the ten years the figure has varied between that high of 58 last year and in 2001 and a low of 36 in 1999. If you take the longer-term view, say over the past thirty years, the increase is far more evident. There were 22 homicides in 1976. That had risen to 35 by 1981. So I think you can say that violent crime has been increasing, steadily, not dramatically. It has really been a case of three steps forward and one or two steps back, depending on the year. However, since the 1970s more and more people have been dying violently and arguably this generation is more violent than the previous one.

What is perhaps more disturbing is not the increase in the figures but the increase in the level of violence associated with these crimes. It is not the number but the type of crimes today that should shock people. In the 1950s, the country would have been convulsed by a case of a farmer shooting another farmer in a row over land. It would have dominated the newspapers for weeks. Today such a crime would make the front page for one day. It now takes something far more tragic, unusual or violent to garner widespread media attention, such as the killing of a child, like the Robert Holohan case last year. There is no doubt that crime is becoming more violent and that is something to worry about it. Tragically, cases where people are attacked and beaten to death on the street for the money in their wallet and their mobile phone are quite common. Liam McGowan was a young man from Kinlough in Co. Leitrim who had only recently started work in an insurance company in Dublin. Four months ago he was attacked in Dublin city centre as he was on his way home from a night out. He subsequently died in hospital. Jimmy Louth, a sixty-six year old man from Cabra, died after he was beaten during a break-in at the bakery he worked in at 3 o'clock in the morning. Three men broke in, tied him and another man up and beat him. What for? To rob a bakery? Why? What was going through the robbers' heads? There was no resistance from Jimmy or the other man. Why did they feel the need to beat him? To hurt him? To harm him to such an extent that very soon afterwards he lost his life.

These are only two recent examples, but they are by no means the most shocking or extreme examples of the type of violent crime that are commonplace in Ireland today. And it is not just in the cities; it is commonplace throughout the country too. You may be familiar with the case of Edward Fitzmaurice, the poor man who was left tied to a chair by a gang who came to rob his shop in Charlestown, Co. Mayo. He later suffocated and died alone. The people who killed him have never been found.

Why?

If we are going to at least try to deal with the increase in violent crime we have to ask ourselves why it is happening. If we can identify the reasons why, then we identify the sources of the problem, thus leading someway towards finding a solution.

It is not rocket science, and in many cases the reasons are obvious and have been for years. In my opinion they are so obvious they have now become clichés.

- *Population increase.* There is more crime in areas where more people live, particularly in the cities and expanding towns.

45

The opposite is also true. There has been a drop in serious crime in areas of declining population. Over the last fifty years, for example in the West and North-West, there has been a drop in the number of killings. This is contrary to the national pattern.

- *Poverty.* It is a well-documented fact that poor people are more likely to end up in trouble with the law and find themselves before the courts and locked in jail. According to a Department of Justice Study on the inmates in Mountjoy Jail (conducted by criminologist Paul O'Mahony) the vast majority of prisoners come from a background and family life of considerable socio-economic and cultural deprivation. Of those in jail, 15 per cent of their fathers had also been incarcerated. Rich people rarely end up in jail, or if they do, rarely end up there for too long. In general, white-collar criminals, if they do appear before the courts, get off with fines, community service or suspended sentences. I'm not saying that rich people should be locked up when they get caught doing something wrong because prison is not always the best form of punishment, but the fact is that poverty is a major cause of crime.

- *Marginalisation/Disadvantage.* Again, it's not just people from particular parts of the country, such as the cities and towns, but those from particular parts of our cities and towns who are more likely to become involved in crime. Again according to this study, the majority of people locked up in Mountjoy jail, 56 per cent, 'came from six very similarly deprived communities in Dublin'. People living in disadvantaged areas with high levels of unemployment, social housing and few educational or recreational facilities are more likely to be involved in crime. Who built, indeed who continues to build, these areas – vast tracts of concrete blocks with no schools, soccer pitches, transport links or community services? Who allows them to continue to be built? Why do we continue to build them when we all know the harm that these environments can do and how hard it is for people to fight against them? Is this a case of profit before people?

- *Education.* A key factor. Too many children are leaving our educational system today without being able to read and write. What are they supposed to do if they haven't got the basic tools of survival? In fact, for many children the schools provide a refuge from the difficulties they experience living in dysfunctional homes in problem areas. It is the only form of routine, security and discipline they know. For some it is the place where they are fed and cleaned, given breakfast and lunch and allowed to have a shower. But our schools close down at 3 p.m. and apart from hosting homework clubs, games and a few community meetings, the facilities there are by and large idle until 9 a.m. the next morning. What a waste of a resource! The latest HSE/Department of Health figures show that 495 children today are homeless because of emotional or behavioural difficulties, the inability of their parents to cope or the abuse of drink and drugs. Most are in their mid to late teens; twenty-two of them are under twelve. Is it beyond our initiative to use at least some of our schools as night-time shelters to feed, clothe and care for kids who have nowhere else to go and who tonight will wander the streets because there is nowhere else for them?

- *Alcohol abuse.* It is something we all know about and have known about for years. A garda report into the causes of crime found that 80 per cent of all crimes are rooted in drink. We see its effects on our streets every night of the week. The main street in many towns and cities in Ireland from midnight to 5 a.m. at the weekends is more akin to something out of the Michael Jackson video, 'Thriller' – without the dancing. Young (and some old) men and women shambling along, drunk as monkeys, shouting, roaring, weaving out in front of cars, falling down, getting sick, urinating in doorways, squabbling and fighting amongst themselves, with others and with the Gardaí, with many sustaining serious injuries and ending up in either a hospital or a morgue. We have all seen the pictures of the A&Es around the country and we all know the major contributor alcohol abuse is to the blockages and the problem of patients on trolleys in casualty departments. It is a clear illustration of one aspect of the changing nature of Irish crime. With the onset of the Celtic Tiger and the fact that people have more money to spend on drink, public order offences have in recent years dramatically increased.

- *Drugs.* This is perhaps the most worrying of the major contributors to crime in Ireland today, not just because of the damage it does to the individuals, their families and their communities and the craving addiction they need to feed which leads them to commit some horrific crimes, but also because of the associated increase in the availability of guns which has made it easier for violent criminals to get hold of them. There has been a drug problem in this country since the early 1970s and indeed heroin and the catastrophic effects it has on individuals and society became very clear in Dublin in the 1980s. But there are a number of factors today that we as a society should really be worried about:

  a the amount of drugs that are coming into Ireland. The Health Research Board estimates it takes over €5 million-worth-a-day to supply the country's recreational users and addicts.

  b the sheer scale of the drugs business – the fact that the seizures are now in the millions and tens of million worth; amounts in the tens and hundreds of thousands barely register. In 1996, Tony Felloni was sent to jail for twenty years after he was caught with €60 thousand-worth of heroin. Today that would almost make him a recreational user – he would probably get a suspended sentence.

  c The amount of money that criminals can make from drug dealing is staggering. Criminal cartels can buy fifty kilos of heroin for just over €1 million. It is worth €10 million on the streets – a ten-fold profit, made very quickly, all in cash.

d   There is now a greater variety of illicit drugs for sale. Once it was cannabis, then LSD and heroin became available. Now the number one drug of choice for dealer and gangland criminal is cocaine. Cocaine, once the preserve of the upper classes, the wealthy who could afford it, is being sold across the social classes. It makes perfect business sense for the drug dealer: the drug is more marketable and it doesn't carry with it the connotations or stigma of heroin. For all intents and purposes it is a cleaner, more sophisticated drug. It is, however, also far more difficult to treat because methadone maintenance does not work with cocaine addicts and consequently it is far more addictive. Ireland has the second highest number of cocaine addicts between the ages of eighteen and twenty-four in the European Union.

- *Guns.* With millions to be made it is not surprising that criminals, particularly those involved in the drug trade, arm themselves to the teeth to protect their empires. The drug trade has provided a conduit for the arms trade as the guns are smuggled in with the consignments. The drug trade has provided a market for the arms dealer because the drug dealers need guns. And the drug trade has not only increased the access to, the availability of and the amount of guns on the streets, it has also increased the variety and lethal capacity of these weapons. Once upon a time criminals used only sawn off shotguns. They still do, but now they also use assault rifles and military weapons, Uzi sub machine guns and pistols. It is not an exaggeration to say the criminals are better armed that the Gardaí and the Army. The favoured weapon among Dublin criminals at the moment is the Glock semi-automatic pistol, a weapon which the Gardaí have sought to use and is only issued to a select few units such as the Emergency Response Unit.

With the increase in and increasing use of firearms, particularly by young men high on cocaine, comes also a consequent disregard for human life. Well-armed criminals with massive drug empires to protect have no qualms about shooting and killing people who get in their way. The variety and quantity of drugs these young people use, along with perhaps the way we as a society have ultimately failed these people, has dulled their consciences and anaesthetised their emotions, as well as their brains. They have become dehumanised, at least for the short time it takes them to raise a gun, point it at another person's head and pull the trigger. Human life is cheapened and no longer sacred. We as a society are sullied and the poorer for it.

- *Gangland.* Criminal gangs don't so much invade as pervade. Individuals form loose alliances, which stick for the purpose of whatever drug deal or other criminal enterprise, such as armed robbery, they are involved in. These gangs establish territories, carve out turf and protect their markets through lethal force. Where shows of strength are needed or perceived slights arise, there was a time when criminals would resort to the fist or the knife. Now they go straight for the gun. That is the situation today in the ongoing drug feuds in Crumlin, Coolock and Limerick. There is of course no loyalty in this business. There is no room for sentiment. Friends are just as ruthlessly, callously and quickly wiped out as enemies.

Well armed, wealthy drug dealing criminals are a focus of fear for law abiding and decent people not just in society in general but in particular in the disadvantaged and marginalised areas in which they operate. But they are also an attraction for the young, ignored, abused, uneducated person in that community who feels he has nothing else going for him. A young man sees a gangster with the gun, the drugs, the money, the jewellery, the tattoos and the girls. He is not looking at a gangster rap music video. He is looking at his neighbour or brother's friend from down the road, or someone he met in

Trinity House [the juvenile detention centre] or someone he shared a cell with in St Patrick's Institution. He is thinking, 'I'll have a piece of that' and he goes for it.

Gangland crime has certainly become a tangible, recognisable and identifiable criminal and societal phenomenon in Ireland. There were always gangs of armed robbers but Irish crime in the past always had its 'Mr Bigs': 'The General' Martin Cahill, 'Factory John' Gilligan, 'The Coach' John Traynor, 'King Scum' Tony Felloni. But the era of the 'Mr Big' is over. Today it's all about the gang; drugs, murder, armed robbery, tiger kidnapping. The individuals involved didn't, unlike those in the past, serve their time. They have just come straight in at the top as drug users, dealers and gunmen. They are younger, more volatile and unstable because many of them also use the drugs they sell and kill or die for. They are extremely violent and more dangerous because they have easy access to firearms and have no compunction about shooting people dead.

- *Juvenile Crime.* The change is very clear to anyone who has been watching the juvenile criminal justice system. Children are now committing more serious crime and coming before the Children's Court charged with more serious offences. They no longer just mitch from school, shoplift or even joyride. Now, along with stealing and crashing high powered cars, armed robbery, theft to order, drug dealing and violent assault are the staples of the Children's Court. More children are also coming before the adult Circuit and Central Criminal Courts because they are committing far more serious crimes such as rape and murder, crimes which are beyond the jurisdiction of the Children's Court.

Two of the three men who shot a uniformed sergeant in the hand and chest at point blank range in Dublin in late September were only sixteen years of age. Like something out of the film *Boyz n the Hood* or other such Hollywood gangster rap movies, they had been driving around in the early hours of the morning in a high powered car with blacked out windows. They had a single barrelled sawn off shotgun which they had used earlier to shoot into a house. They came back to that house at 6 o'clock that morning and when Sgt Mark Clarke took off his hat and approached the car, they rolled down the driver's electronic window, pushed the gun out and fired at him. Luckily he turned sideways and the hat under his arm took some of the force of the blast. He's lucky to be alive. They didn't care that he was a Garda. They were high on cocaine. One of the sixteen-year-olds had to be taken to hospital after he was arrested because he had overdosed.

Tragically it is no longer unusual to turn on the radio and hear that a man has been shot dead in a drug or gangland killing in Dublin, Waterford, Limerick, Cork or even Clare. One of the best-known and longest established criminal gangs in the country is based in West Clare. People have been murdered up the mountains; young men have been dumped in canals or buried in forests. They have been tortured, stabbed, dismembered, disposed of, never to be heard of again, missing, presumed dead. Gangland murder is now a fact of Irish life.

On the international stage Irish criminals are also playing their part. Ex-pat criminals based in the UK, Holland and Spain, for example, have formed alliances with Turkish heroin wholesalers in London, South American cocaine suppliers and Moroccan cannabis dealers in Spain. They are as astute and as ruthless as the rest of their criminal counterparts. They have reaped the ill-gotten gains but many too have paid the price for their involvement with their lives. The chopped-up body of 38-year-old drug dealer Michael 'Dancer' Aherne from Cork was found in a fridge in an apartment on the Algarve. The infamous and psychopathically violent Westies, Stephen Sugg and Shane Coates, West Dublin drug dealers who terrorised many people in Whitestown, Hartstown and Blanchardstown, were murdered and buried under concrete in an industrial estate on the Costa Blanca.

It is a pretty bleak and depressing picture. The reality is that the situation we find ourselves in today is, I believe, really one of our own making. The fact is that every gangland killing is a testament to our failure as individuals and as a society. It is a failure to care for our fellow citizens, a failure to give them the same chances that we got ourselves, a failure to give them the same reasons as we had for not ending up in their situation in life.

Live by the Sword, Die by the Sword

There is a theory that abounds at the moment and it goes along the lines of 'if you live by the sword you die by the sword'. People might say these people are killing each other, so let them at it. There will be less of them for us to worry about, they're all scumbags, drug dealers and killers anyway so let them off to shoot, wound, mutilate, torture and kill each other. Why should we worry – you live by the sword, you die by the sword. But this is the wrong attitude for many reasons, and here's two: if you subscribe to that theory, then you go on to create monsters which at some stage you will no longer be able to control. You will inculcate in these people a sense of invincibility to go along with the sense of invulnerability they already feel they have. They are young, fit, fast, strong, active and in many cases full of drugs. They are very volatile, unstable and violent. They have no problem killing each other and if you allow them to continue to do so, it won't be long before they start killing you and people like you. They won't distinguish. They will kill anyone that gets in their way. At the moment it is rival drug dealers, but next it could be the garda who arrests them, the solicitor or barrister who prosecutes them, the judge who locks them up, the prison officer who wants to keep them locked up. One of these could be your father, mother, brother, sister, friend, lover or even you. They may even want to kill the journalist who writes about them. They already did it once before in 1996 when they shot Veronica Guerin dead. Innocent people – even children – can get caught in the crossfire.

In many ways this first reason is almost a selfish reason, one of self-preservation. Stop them, get them, because if you don't they'll get you and yours. It is legitimate, practical, perhaps not very moral or altruistic, but in reality short-term thinking. The second reason however is, I believe, far more valid and forward thinking: these gangland killers and drug dealers are not aliens. They didn't come down from another planet. They are people, young men and women who, a few years ago before the drugs and the insanity kicked in, looked just like you and me. A few years before that they were adorable little baby boys and girls who cried and laughed and wet their nappies and drank their bottles just like you and I did. However, when they fell, nobody picked them up and held them. When they laughed, nobody cared. When they cut their knees, no one gave them a plaster. They didn't always get a bottle when they cried, more than likely they got a wallop, that's if Daddy and Mammy were around and not out drinking, taking drugs or locked up in prison. And by and large they didn't have anyone to get them up in the morning, wash them, ensure they had clean clothes, get them to school, make sure they stayed there and learned, and check their homework when they came home. They certainly didn't have anyone to take them to Irish dancing, music or swimming classes after school and pay for an ice cream or a bar of chocolate for them on the way home. In short these people did not get the same love, care, or social and educational opportunities that all of us here did. They didn't get the same chance. They were marginalised and criminalised. They found their sense of belief, belonging, worth, livelihood and leisure in the gang. And guns, drugs and violence are all part of that way of life.

How do you tackle that? I'm no expert but it seems to me that if you radically interfere you can make a difference. The cliché, tackle crime by tackling the causes of crime, is a truism. It seems to me that if you tackle the problems of poverty, disadvantage, marginalization and in particular the lack of education and opportunity, you could go a long way towards putting people like me out of a job.

Interculturalism:

Ireland
of the
Welcomes?

A View from the Chair

Cian O'Síocháin

The section of the Céifin conference which I chaired was entitled 'Interculturalism: Ireland of the Welcomes?' I was especially pleased that the question mark was included as it gave us an opportunity to consider an issue that does tend to be ignored in modern Ireland. The issue in question is the elephant in the room of our economically thriving nation. The economists tell us that we need many thousands of immigrants to keep our economy buoyant, but how do we treat, interact with and feel about those who come to live and work here? Generally when the issues are touched upon in the Irish media it will take the form of an Irish panel of journalists, politicians and analysts discussing Irish attitudes. There are rarely present representatives of the communities to give us the view from the inside. The actual humanity of our immigrant population is rarely conveyed to the Irish public at large. The immigrant community in Ireland is generally faceless, nameless and ultimately nothing more than a vague concept inadequately conveyed with words. Stripped of their humanity, economic migrants can morph in the mind's eye into a threat or menace of one kind or another. Certain publications feed these kinds of fears and as a result many people in Ireland have inadvertently slipped into an unconscious mistrust.

The word 'welcome' itself can be deceiving. You are 'welcome' into my home to clean it is very different from you are 'welcome' into my home to spend time with myself and my family. It is a subtle yet vital difference and gives us a clearer vision of exactly what kind of welcome we have extended. The economy's voracious appetite for unskilled labour has left us with a difficulty with regard to integration. This was highlighted very clearly by the kinds of questions put forward by the conference delegates. They were exploratory in a way that indicated many people had never interacted with an immigrant before. It must be said that in many cases people would not have had an opportunity like that presented by the conference, and herein lies the true value of this section.

I tend to associate the phrase 'Ireland of the Welcomes' with the tourist industry. The major difference between tourists and immigrants is that tourists go home. We have, for many years, swelled the coffers of the economy with the spending of our visitors but we seem less comfortable with the wider social realities of people who bring economic benefits but also put down roots. While the great benefits of simply speaking to people on a human level cannot be measured, there is a dearth of opportunity for the population in general to interact with people in a way afforded to those who attended this year's Céifin conference. While there might be a will on the part of some sectors of the population to address this, it can be said with certainty that most people will not make any effort to interact with the immigrant population. In the aftermath of the section the delegates were quick to point out the benefits of interaction and discussion on the issue of interculturalism, and many spoke of the insight they had gained into the reality of being an immigrant in modern Ireland. I couldn't help noticing, however, that nobody seemed to bat an eyelid at the conference dinner when it became clear that it was an almost exclusively immigrant workforce that served the food. It is clear that, at this year's Céifin conference, the issue was tackled but only in an exploratory way. There remains much work to be done in this area. This work has a good grounding in the question which was teased out at this year's conference: Ireland of the Welcomes?

Telling My Story

Dr Katherine Chan Mullen [China]

I finished my studies in 1978, I married an Irish man and I came to Ireland. I see how Ireland has changed. I see how the air has changed. I can see lots of changes. We were the first Chinese society in Ireland. We brought the Dublin Mayor, the first to bring a Dublin Mayor, to China. I was the first person to bring the Irish Ceolthas, the Irish traditional singing and dance, to China – long before the River Dancers! Also I was the first person to set up a free Chinese Information Centre for the Irish people and Chinese people. Also, I am quite proud of being awarded, the first Chinese person awarded, by the City Council and the Mayor one of Dublin's 'Unsung Heroes' awards. Of course, this is the first time a Chinese person has been invited as a speaker to a Céifin conference. I feel very proud!

I want to say that I love Ireland, whatever it is, even the crime, even the drugs, even anything. That's most important, because that love makes me speak here today. I thought I would talk to only twenty or thirty people. So now I talk to hundreds of people and I am really scared!

After the Polish community, we are the second biggest community; of this everybody is aware. I came here in the summer of 1971. The sky was always grey, no sunshine, very little sunshine. And the winter was very, very cold and very long. But the people had a very warm heart. That made up for it.

What was different at that time was that there was no McDonalds, there was no Chinese supermarket. I couldn't buy instant noodles. I would have to get a boat all the way to London to get something to eat! Also, there was very little crime; on the newspaper I never see a robbery or somebody being killed. There were only three Chinese restaurants: one on Exchequer Street and two on O'Connell Street: one is called the 'Lula Restaurant', next to the Gresham Hotel. The other is called 'The Sunflower', right beside the bridge; now is called 'Burger King'.

I was a College of Surgeons student. I did one year there, then I changed. I could walk from Trinity College Library at 10 p.m. and afterwards go to a party alone as a little girl (I am still not that big) and walk along O'Connell Street back to where I stayed in Gardiner Street. You know how dirty Gardiner Street is today; those days Gardiner Street was also full of drunkards. The worst they would do is hug you, that's all. They wouldn't hit you, they wouldn't rob your handbag. I walked every day, every night, I never had a fare. But today it is totally different. I find that Irish weather is getting warmer, more sunshine and no snow in the winter. But Irish people's hearts are getting cooler. It was warm heart, cold weather. Now it's cooler heart, warmer winter.

I think the problem is with the way Chinese come each year from 1999. In 1998 our Taoiseach went to China and then the Tánaiste went to China, open armed, and said, 'Please, come to Ireland to study. You are more than welcome'. So thousands each month, three thousand students each month come to Ireland to study. Each one bring €10,000 minimum, minimum, and that only lasts for six months because €5,000/6,000 goes into the school, another few thousand into the very high cost of living. So then they found out that Ireland is not what you expect from website or newspaper. They expect to find the friendly people, lovely weather and everything is cheap. But it is not the case.

We are faced with the same problem here [as the Polish].
Chinese come here for slightly different reasons than our friends
because we come here not as refugees. We are not here just seeking
jobs. When I first came here, there were very few Chinese, only 200
people in 1971. Of course today there is unofficially 80,000 to
90,000 Chinese in Ireland and I would say that most work hard.
They make money through their work. There is no government
grant for them at all. Chinese are very embarrassed to ask for social
welfare even though they are entitled to it. Even if they paid twenty
years' tax, they never ask for social welfare. Government, they
forgot about the Chinese, because we don't have any grant from the
government at all. But Irish people are generous, very generous. So
we got the grants and the help from Irish people.

Apart from these differences between us, we are all
immigrants, even now I am married to an Irish man. I have Irish
passport. I am still considered an immigrant, old immigrant, not
new. We face the same problems. The first one we face is the
high cost of living. For just €1 in China you can buy so many
things. You come here you couldn't even buy one bottle of Coca
Cola. That's why students go mad seeking jobs. We have
competition here with my friends from Poland. The Chinese
students are fighting for the jobs. Not everyone has their
working permit; students are only allowed twenty hours' work
now. Some students don't even have twenty hours. So there is a
big problem facing all the Chinese community.

Second thing is the increasing crime. That also causes lots and
lots of problems for people. It's bad for young people to be always
in the pub. My son was in UCD; I know exactly what the life is
like. He couldn't get out of the pub: meeting in the pub, eating in
the pub, talking and girlfriend all in the pub. So alcohol is a big
problem. It is alcohol plus drugs that kill you. The Chinese are not
used to this. So that is why I set up this Chinese Information
Centre to teach the Chinese that the Irish people are lovely, but
once they have the alcohol plus the drugs they are not lovely. In
2003 a Chinese man walked to Beaumont Street to buy a four

pack of beer. There were two sixteen-year-old kids who must have been on drugs. As they are teasing, they are saying, 'You are Chinese, what are you doing here?' so he is teasing back and the sixteen-year-old just grabbed one of the iron bars from the side without thinking and hit this man's head. He died immediately on Beaumont Road. That was in 2003 and that young man, because he was underage, got only eighteen months in jail. And the mother and father nearly committed suicide because of that dead man. The punishment is too low in Ireland. You see in Japan or in China, punishment for theft is severe; if they injure somebody, it might be death penalty. So in Japan or in China, you don't steal. In Ireland you're a thief, you get six weeks, a television in the room, €2.50 per week pocket money. Then six weeks, out, you steal again. The Chinese man, you may remember, killed by a thief last May: he heard his girlfriend downstairs call 'Help', came down and was knifed in the liver and bled to death. The penalty for this here is too low.

I also agree that racism is rising. One day in Bewley's Hotel an old lady, beautiful dress, big diamond ring on her finger, said to me, 'What are you doing here? This is our Dublin, you should go back to China.' I said, 'Lady, I paid twenty-eight years' high tax in this country, and what were you Irish doing in New York for those years?' She could not answer, she ran away. So just to say, Irish people have to face that this is the multicultural world now. You can't be the exception, so you have to face up to how to educate our young people. Bring back Irish people's love.

Cian O'Síocháin I'll now ask Adam to say a few words.

Adam Rogalinski [Poland]
My name is Adam Rogalinski. I am one of the many Poles around. There is about 200,000 of us around Ireland. That's an official number, but it might be more, might be less. I arrived here five years ago. I lived in Greece as well as in Germany. I enjoyed both but not as much as Ireland. I did hotel management and it brought me to Liscannor just down the road

five years ago to the CERT course for bartenders. I got the placement in Kerry, one of the most beautiful parts of your country, in a five-star hotel where I stayed for two-and-a-half years. I met a couple of famous people including the Taoiseach, a lovely man, except he kept me very late in the bar!

Then the opportunity arose to go back to Clare, again just down the road in Lahinch. I enjoyed my time there for one year but my feet brought me again up north. I'm in Galway now where I work in a couple of places. I work in GMIT. That's how I got here and at the moment I am back in the off-licence business. From this I can say a few things about the abuse of alcohol. Being in the off-licence business, it shows you how big a problem it is here and how drink affects people. Doctors here mentioned that the rate [of alcohol abuse] in Ireland is going up. From my experience in the country, it is not only the young people, it's the thirty- and forty-year olds that very often emigrated to the US, Australia, and have come back after years. The drink changed people very much. I have been a bar manager for a couple of years and just for refusing to serve drink I am told, 'Go back to your country'. But I don't want you to get the impression that I am upset. It is just a minority of people. I am not saying that the Polish are perfect. We are far from it. We are not the most tolerant people in the world. But I love Ireland itself and I love the Irish people. I love the way you live, your Sunday lunches, your carveries, your bacon and cabbage and pint with it. It is great. It is part of your history and Polish coming over here, they might have problems with adjusting to you, the society, and understanding the way you live. I look at it from the perspective that this is the way you grew up. Your parents coming down for the Sunday lunch and you coming with them, playing pool.

The problem I find in Ireland at the moment would be the 200,000 Poles. No matter how many Polish people there are around Ireland it is hard to get them socialised with the Irish. I am sure in most places there is some Polish person. Maybe you know they're from Krakow, but do you know anything else about them? The problem is that Irish society is not as open as it could be. You opened your borders, fair play, and we don't have to apply any more for visas and work permits. It is absolutely fantastic and both nations benefit from that. But we are both thinking of huge benefit. As Dr Mullen said, Chinese very often come over here to study. I won't lie, we are coming here to make money, same as the Irish were doing in the US. Most of us will go back home eventually. Some of us might stay. I am here five years and, to be fair, I still don't know what I am going to do, take a mortgage for €300 grand? Doesn't sound too encouraging.

But this country is an absolutely fantastic place with great opportunities. Taking myself as an example, starting here as a trainee bartender, going up as a bar manager, duty manager and then deputy catering manager in GMIT, I think I wouldn't get this sort of chance back home in Poland, although I feel Polish 100 per cent and I think Poland is a fantastic country and I really hope that things will turn around as they did in Ireland. I just want to say that if the Irish can stay the way they are and just maybe try to get the Polish more involved in the local communities. I play soccer for one of the local teams in Knocknacarra and for twenty-six players that are on the team I am the only one [Pole]. So it's taking the opportunity and involving people in sport that I think is one of the first steps that will get the Polish and Irish mixed together, because we do have the same culture and we are all Catholics, well, most of us, including myself. We both share the same passions. We all love soccer. Well, except maybe when the Irish team doesn't play that well. They'll get there eventually!

Both nations had a very hard time in history. You got a hard time from the English. We got it from the Russians and from the Germans and then from the Russians again. I suppose if things go on as they are at the moment there is a great, great opportunity that the friendship between the Irish and Polish will grow, and not only mixing between the Irish boys picking up the Polish girls but more people getting involved in everything else.

Cian O'Síocháin I'll now ask Salome to say a few words.

Salome Mbugua Henry [Kenya]
My name is Salome Mbugua. I live in Portarlington, Co. Offaly, and this is what I tell people when they ask where I am from. I am originally from Kenya, and Portarlington is definitely not in Kenya! I was baptised by an Irish priest and actually most African people have high respect for Irish people, mainly because of the experience with the religious priests and nuns who have done tremendous work and continue to do tremendous work in Africa. I arrived in Ireland in 1994. I have seen three faces of Ireland since I have been here and I will talk about them in a minute. I have been involved in working with homeless young people in Dublin 1 and it was actually quite exciting working with them in the capacity of a social worker. I had one child who used to call me 'my black African mother'. Then I moved to work with women and I actually found it very encouraging to work with Irish women because we shared the same kind of discrimination, apart from colour. Just moving to Ireland, I found it welcoming. I found the culture shocking but people were very friendly. People would say 'Hello' to you. I used to go line dancing. I did a lot of line dancing. I even won a cup!

But coming back to 1994, we did so many activities with the students, visiting homes and sleeping over and such kind of things. Coming back in 1998, things had really changed, the attitude had really hardened. People weren't as welcoming as they were before. I was a victim of racism, both physical and verbal, which has been very common. So I just see it as something that I need to challenge and to speak about. I shared experiences with other people and it actually became very easy for many people to talk about their experiences as well. As you know, what you see about Africa is very negative. But Africa is a rich continent. It has beautiful people. I don't know how many of you have visited Africa to see the beauty of it. I was actually going into many supermarkets the other day just to see what imported African food they had, and they had some from Kenya. Here in Ireland we are importing oil from Nigeria as well.

This week is Anti-Racist Week in the Workplace. I would like to quote research I was involved in: 41 per cent of Irish people are still very racist. The most negative attitude is towards black African people. And again it goes back to the stereotyping. Also, there is a tendency for people to believe that the majority of the people here are asylum seekers and again they are seeing the colour and thinking that all the black people who are here are asylum seekers. Today I am speaking from my own experience, but also as a representative of my people, as well as in the capacity of Director of the African Women's Network in Ireland [AkiDwA]. We have brought social workers from South Africa and even some doctors. We have many doctors from Sudan, Pakistan and everywhere else that don't have a good experience, yet they are contributing to this society. It is all about the attitude.

Coming back to 2003 the whole thing changes again and we have seen people actually advocating for people who have been deported to be brought back to Ireland. So I have seen changes and it is very difficult for me at this time and age to be able to tell you what is going on so it still has not become clear. But I think it is the fear of the unknown. The fear of the stranger that you don't know or a person that is out there and what they may do to you. That fear is out there, but as well the generalisation. I am talking about Africa and African people and the majority of them are here to stay.

I also want to talk very quickly about an organisation that we founded in 2001, which I am representing today: AkiDwA. In 2001, I actually mobilised a group of women to come together and discuss our experiences of Ireland. We had a sense of isolation in common. Growing up and living in Africa, a child is brought up by the whole community. And yet when people came here, they didn't know anybody and so the attitude and environment wasn't very welcoming. When we came together we talked about our isolation. We talked about our experiences of physical and verbal attack. We spoke about our domestic violence within our own marriages. We actually asked to be given the opportunity to speak for ourselves and the majority of African women have been speaking for themselves. But before they can do that, we have to give them training. Apart from all that, racism was a major issue that we had to challenge in this country and I actually found a lot of confidence. I don't shy away and I don't hide and I actually face people when they become racist in a very calm way. Some people don't know that they are being very racist. And the first thing was to give the women the training to be able to go and reach schools, to be able to reach the women's groups, to talk about themselves and the issues that are affecting them. The Irish Country Women's Association, like in Athlone, have been very supportive of migrant women, especially African women. And many other support groups have come together to help many migrant women and really we owe them a big deal if we are to make changes in this changing Ireland.

There are other issues that I may not be able to get through as there are so many. But again to say, women are very happy to be asked, 'Why did you leave your country, why did you come here?' I am very confident talking about myself, but not everybody would like to be reminded of the trauma and what they have gone through. We have people who have come from Rwanda who went through the genocide and left even during the war. I don't know whether you have heard, but about 67 per cent of the 5,000 women who left during the genocide are HIV positive. We have some of those women living here with us. They have not been able to access proper services. We are living with women who are victims of trauma and torture and not even being able to receive services. We have asylum seekers who are living in deprivation, in what we call an 'open prison system'. We have asylum seekers who have to sign on in the morning before they can be allowed to leave the room and yet we talk of freedom? We actually have denied people the right to work and that is why there is a very negative attitude about black people, because everybody assumes they are asylum seekers. But if they are not given the opportunity to work, yet they are ready to work, what will happen?

I was going to talk about what we did with the women who don't want to be asked why they came to this country. We published a book, *Her Story*, in January 2006 and it is actually very telling in relation to migration of African women to Ireland, why they left their countries, the experience of their migration journey. But, most importantly, it gives you a clear understanding. We have cases of women who were jailed, raped in prison, women who were mutilated, female genital mutilation and many other things. We didn't bring many copies, we only brought ten copies, but we have around 1,000 in the office and it would be important for people to even inform themselves of what has happened to some of these women. Their lives have been very damaged and some of them may never be able to recover.

Something that I would like to see happening and I will actually ask all of us to work for and think about is integration: not just about buying fair food and bringing people together to chat. Integration is about giving people better jobs and also helping them to be able to do what they can in order to get out of that isolation So actually we are a long way to integration, we are a long way to meeting the needs of our newcomers or people who are coming into this country. But most of all, migrants, especially women, in this country lack the support of networks that they were used to in their own countries. I request that we be able to support these people. So what I have given you is nothing actually of what I would have seen in the last twelve years but, because of time, I'll leave it there and I really would like to thank you for listening to me.

Cian O'Síocháin Finally, we will hear from Nilton.

Jose Nilton Vieira de Souza [Brazil]
As Brazilians, of course we didn't come here to learn football! I am living here for the last four-and-a-half years. I came straight

to Oranmore where I worked for three-and-a-half years in a hotel, which I really enjoyed, met lots of great people there. As you see, my English is not perfect, but I learned my English in the hotel. I have never been in a class to learn English before so whatever I say here today I am sorry if it is not clear but I will try my best to answer your questions after.

I lived here two years on my own. I left my wife and my daughter in Brazil. Then when I felt like I was well settled with some English, with some money, I bring them to live with me. About work permits, I do have a work permit but my wife is not allowed to work so I have to work double to keep them, to keep my rent, to keep my food, to keep my car. At the same time, I do loads of volunteer work in the community. You might see [in the news] in the last few weeks, in the last few months, about Gort community, where we live. We have many projects there like football, music. We do really have a good integration with the community there. I have asked a few business people if they want Brazilians to stay there: they say yes. They don't want us to leave Gort because the town has changed. And they really like us. I feel support in the Gort community. But there are loads of things that can be changed, loads of things to be done, especially with people who don't have any English. The average age there it is about thirty-five and the majority there are men so they really find it hard to learn English.

Most people come [here] from one certain state in Brazil: Goyaz. The government in Brazil doesn't really look after those people there. They are not investing money, they are not giving enough for education and they are not giving enough for unemployment. So they have lots of difficulties to get here. And when they get here they have to figure out where to go. That is where myself and another three or four people, who also work as volunteers, try to help them. In 2004 we did a development course in Gort. So there was myself and another three Brazilians girls studying with twenty-four Irish people. So it was a good moment to get to know the community, to get to know what they are doing and to show our interest to be there. Of course, it is to earn some money, but not only money. From my point of view, if we can come to this country to get some money and learn English, definitely in our country people who speak English will get good jobs. So we hopefully will get some funding some day to keep our Brazilian association open there because it is all in a volunteer capacity and no one gets paid. I give twenty-five hours a week free. There are a lot of people there who give thirty-five hours a week free for those people. So if we stop helping them, who looks after them? People who find it hard filling in forms, getting a provisional licence, or anything. I am not looking for congratulations. I know we do a great job. No one can come and complain about us because we do have the trust from the community there. One thing to remember is that there are twenty-seven groups in the community and we are very well involved with them. Another thing I would say is that we are active with football; we had a Brazilian football team this year here in Co. Clare where we won the competition (I forgot the name of the town). We do have people out there working, trying to show people our music, our samba, and even today here after dinner we are going to have our girls from the group play some samba for you all. I hope you can shake your bodies just a little bit!

Being a volunteer has changed my life completely. You are never going to find someone who will give you some money to be a volunteer or somebody who will come and say your community needs this or that. So someone in the community – two or three or four or five, ten people – has to see what needs to be done. If you do have time, talk to people to see if they are happy, if there is any disease, if there are any psychological problems or anything, anything. I am sure every community has problems so if you give just three hours, two hours from your time and be a volunteer, I am sure loads of things will change. And I am sure you are always going to find people to support what you do. Hopefully when I go back to my country some day I will do there what I learned here. She asked me not to mention her name, but Dr Niamh

Clune is one of the most important people in Gort at the moment. She is doing a great job and she is supporting all the community. She has many skills and she is organising all those twenty-seven groups in Gort and getting people together, getting the groups together. Everyone has to be on the same boat, do the same thing, and I am sure Gort, with her ideas, is going to be a model for an integration community in this Irish society some day. I am sure that will happen. Gort has become very famous and, I am sure, will be more famous than we are at the moment.

Questions & Answers
Cian Adam, do you feel that sport is a good way to integrate other nationalities into society in Ireland?

Adam Absolutely, Cian. I have been involved with girls' soccer down in GMIT. I was a trainer. I did a couple of sessions with them. As I said before, not all the Poles or any other foreigners in this country can speak English well enough just to go down to the pub and start chatting to other people. Sport, especially soccer, is this sort of event where you really don't have to talk, you just pass the ball. It builds some sort of connection between the people, and playing with the guys there are laughs, jokes about the Poles eating the swans from the river. Just to make it clear, we don't eat swans back home! I think sport is the best way to get to the people.

Cian I am delighted that *Her Story* was published because I think a lot of Irish people would be very interested. Maybe it is a cultural thing, but in many cases, when an Irish person asks an African woman where they are from and why they have come to this country, it is really in an effort to be helpful. I can imagine how there might be an element of racism in us all. We know the Chinese come to study in many cases, the Poles come to work and the Brazilians come because of Gort. But Africa is such a large country and I speak for myself when I say that I don't know much about the African story. There are people from Sierra Leone, Kenya, Nigeria, and I honestly would like to know the story. I think if people were more aware of the African story, there may well be less racism. Now people will always be racist. It's just I feel that it is such a vast continent. If the African story became more public, I think there would be more understanding as such. Salome, would you respond to that?

Salome This is where we have the problem because there is the generalisation out there, reinforced by the media. 'They' must be coming to look for something. But actually the statistics are down. Asylum seekers number only 3 per cent. We have people who are here as teachers from Africa, we have social workers. We have psychiatric nurses working in the prison and Portlaoise hospital. Go to any hospital, Tullamore where I live or Portlaoise, and you will see the majority of the doctors and nurses there are foreign. Yes, Africa is a poor continent and you will see even from this book [*Her Story*] that people come here for all those other reasons: economic or political. So it's a mixture, but whether you are a doctor or not, you are still an asylum seeker in the eyes of many Irish people. They are misinformed. They rely on the generalisation, on what they have seen or what they have heard.

Q. I don't know whether the following question is answerable or not. Could I ask each of the panel to complete the sentence, 'If I knew then what I know now ...'?

Katherine We learned very little, but in the last ten years there is a lot more information about Ireland. Back then my father didn't know where Ireland was. We looked over the whole map. I said, 'Dad, it is there'. He said, 'Never heard about this country'. We only heard about the UK. We still thought Ireland was part of UK. But these days, there are lots of websites and books, and we did culture exchanges with Beijing. Ireland wins the number one best environment country to live in, number one in the Far East last year. The air is good, the weather is good (I keep talking about the weather!) and the people are friendly. Forgive me if I spoke about the bad things. Chinese still love

Ireland more than other countries. It is all good news about Ireland but it is still not enough.

Adam I'd love to see Polish people being as proud of being Polish as the Irish are proud because they are Irish, because of their nation. I would love to see Polish being so proud of their own country.

Salome For me, it's the distance. Before I came here I worked in Uganda and Uganda is very near my country so it was just like dropping from one county to the other. I find it hard being away from home but apart from that I have great friends and I know great people. I know the Irish are great people as well, but there are those few. It's still great to be here.

Nilton I love a few drinks and I feel this country is very safe. I think there is a lot of crime but there is not as much as we have in our country. I feel at home here and I do not plan to go back maybe for the next five or ten years. My wife does not like when I say this as she wants to go back as soon as possible to be with her family. But I like what I am doing and I like the people I work with and I know myself that I do have a lot of things to learn and I'm sure the knowledge I bring from this country some day will help my community, will help my town, will help my country.

Katherine I forgot to say a very important thing. The Irish people have great charity and great heart. I will give you an example. I was working in a transfusion bank in Hong Kong. There you have to pay the people who give blood. But in Ireland people queue for days to give blood to save other people's lives. That was the first thing that warmed my heart.

Comment from the floor I am involved with an organisation called the Lions Clubs of Ireland at committee level. We have 115 clubs and we are very anxious to have interaction and contact with groups that are settling here. The purpose of the organisation is to serve the needs of the community. I will be around for the conference and I'd be only delighted to have a chat with any of the groups that are here because we are keen to know where we can help.

Comment from the floor Mine is by way of comment rather than question, but I had the privilege of living in Kenya for a couple of years. The thing that struck me coming back to Ireland from working as a missionary in Kenya was that people asked me, 'how did you like it, tell us about it'. But as soon as I began to tell them they moved onto a different subject. I often feel that while we are curious as a people, our interest in the other person's story quickly dies. On the other hand I found in Kenya a tremendous interest on the part of the people there in what we were about here. Finding out about farming, about the way of life. That whole way of life that has changed in Ireland, in that we depend on the supermarket, and so on.

Q. It is precisely the question of culture. We have heard about sport, pubs, but it seems to me that one of the very enriching possibilities for encounter between different cultures is precisely in different cultural events. I am just wondering if the members of the panel or the people they represent have found their way into Irish cultural events apart from the pub? How do they invite Irish people to share in their cultural events and be enriched by their culture?

Nilton In our community, we do help Irish people and Brazilian people join together for music as well as soccer. About a week ago we had the Cooley Collins Festival in Gort. It is a very important festival and we were invited to play our music there and do our dance. And on that day I got an idea from one person there, an Irish person, who asked if our group could mix the Irish dance with the Brazilian music, especially with the samba. And very soon we will be talking about that and we will get Irish music or Irish dance, Brazilian music or Brazilian dance together all the time.

Salome I have actually even seen it in Dublin where the priest would give the Mass in African. So it is not even about sharing food, dances. Apart from that, in the African Women's Network we have held many cultural events where we portrayed our culture, our music, our food and other Kenyan produce. So we too ask Irish people to share with us.

Adam There are a couple of shops around Galway selling Polish food. Even when I arrived in Ireland the only place you could buy Polish beer was a shop down in Shannon. From Kenmare to Shannon is a fair bit of a drive but we did it a couple of times. But at this stage you go anywhere else you get a great selection of Polish beers, Polish vodkas. I have seen lately the Irish boys buying Soviesky, one of the Polish vodkas. So there is a change in the market. There are Polish Masses in Galway as well, twice a month. I have been there once or twice but I haven't seen any Irish there. It is hard to blame them because the Polish language is difficult enough. There are a couple of famous rock bands coming over from Poland to play a couple of gigs in Galway. So there is a bit of cultural mixture, although I think it is not enough. There is space to improve things.

Katherine The Chinese are part of the Chinese restaurants. We do have the Chinese Information Centre since 2002. We have line dance classes. We have Chinese basketball and Chinese football teams, and we are willing to include young Irish people too. Also we had two very famous Chinatown festivals in Dublin. One was in Smithfield in 2004, the other in Collins Barracks. This was the integration of the Irish culture and the Chinese culture. We give out free books in Smithfield Centre. We are open Monday to Friday. We have a lot of Chinese cultural things there. You are more than welcome to come in, chat in Chinese, learn some Chinese or read a book and have a cup of coffee. Not Irish coffee, just ordinary coffee!

Q. To go back to a comment from the floor that there is a bit of racism in us all, I would have to disagree. We have prejudices but I would have to challenge the idea that we are all racist. I would ask the four speakers, is it a challenge of integration versus diversity? How do both projects mesh at ground level? How do we influence policy development, or should it be a mixture of different things? At the last count there was 187 different nationalities living in Ireland. With the best will in the world, the resources aren't there to support our own minority groups, like Travellers etc., so how are we going to deal and engage and integrate? Is integration the right way? Is that what the communities want or would they prefer a different way?

Nilton I was trying to explain before, there is now a group called Grace and in that group we do have a plan for the future. A minimum of one person represents each group in Grace. This is an important idea, an important project to get all the community to learn English and on an adequate amount of money. As has been said before, to live and spend is really hard. So we are trying to raise funds. We do have a volunteer who has a degree in English. His name is Iasouva and he has great English and is working very hard for the community. We do have another Brazilian who has a degree in English and we have two priests in the community who lived in Brazil for a few years and both speak great Portuguese. So for us, it is all involved in language. If we do not get the language, we are not going to get anywhere. One other thing, it is really serious stuff, not only in Gort, but throughout the country. There is a need for a proper interpreting service because we heard that someone died in Galway, a Polish person I heard, and they didn't have anyone to explain to the family what had happened. So they got a person from the cleaner who had some English to explain what had happened. That happened in Gort also. Sometimes kids go with the parents to the doctor to translate and sometimes it is very personal information, or sometimes it is a young girl explaining to her father what is wrong. There is a big need in this country for a proper interpreting service. Without that we are not going to get anywhere.

Salome Integration is a real challenge for Ireland. First, it is to acknowledge the diversity, that we come from different backgrounds, we have our own ways of life. But as well as respecting that, if we are really going to integrate people, does it mean that we put in an education system with a syllabus reflecting only the background of this country? Integration should not just be a one-way thing. It should be looked at in the wider perspective, even re-training teachers from this background so they can be within the education system, so that children can identify with them and with children from those backgrounds. That is the real challenge. But the most important thing is to acknowledge diversity and to respect diversity. If we can't acknowledge diversity, then it would be very hard to work on integration.

Comment from the floor I just would like to return to the Gort story and mention the fact that the Brazilian festival in Gort this year was excellent. I would propose the idea of a celebration or festival where Irish people can get to know more about their new neighbours. Each town where there is an ethnic group would put on a festival on a yearly basis or, perhaps, more often, with the help of some monies from the local council. In Gort, it is 'Gort of the Generosity', *go néirí an einí*. It is a very good starting point. I would recommend strongly that Céifin make this approach to the various councils.

Comment from the floor I think if we want to deal with racism we really have to begin with the children. Racism is a learned thing. During research as a teacher and as a researcher, I had a class of twenty-nine children in a circle and the topic for discussion was 'Should this family be deported?' I had a large picture from *The Irish Times* in the middle of the floor of Mrs Ojay from Nigeria who had failed in her asylum case. Initially everybody said, 'Well, you know, Ireland is a very small country, if we let in every hard case, we will be swamped'. And I didn't intervene because I am the facilitator, but by the time it had run on for forty-five minutes there wasn't a single child who thought they should be deported. Because the more they looked, the more they empathised with the humanity of the person. As soon as they looked at the humanity of the situation, the child in its mother's arms, the thinking changed.

Comment from the floor For two summers we have had the Open Door Intercultural Festival in Cork and we are hoping to run one again next year. This year we had thirteen nationalities. It was a family festival, so we had children's games, we had food, we had toys and we had singing and music. So if anyone is interested in the festival for next year, could they come to the Eastern European and Ireland Association stand.

Comment from the floor I just wanted to say that as much as we are talking about integration we have to know that it is two-way traffic. The immigrants, as the immigrants, have to make the move. I am speaking in respect to some talks I did in a primary school. You know, kids are very innocent. We could enlighten them and mobilise them to tell them why there are immigrants here. This is a new Ireland. Many people think that if you are black and in Ireland you are a refugee or asylum seeker. But it is two-way traffic. We have to make a move, the Irish as well. We have to make a move to make a change.

Comment from the floor The panel are giving a feeling that the Irish are becoming more racist. I would like to think that those committing verbal or physical abuses are in the minority. But would you agree that it is not only the Irish that are becoming more racist, it is also these communities as well?

Salome I want to say that the Irish are not becoming more racist. In 2001 it was 52 per cent. In 2006, it has dropped to 41 per cent. We are not saying that they are becoming more racist. We are saying racism is still there. People still continue to experience racism. I don't have a list but I have not come across anybody who has been abused or attacked by any migrant. Maybe they are there but I have not come across it.

Katherine I don't think racism is the biggest problem for our immigrants. It is drug abuse and the violence. But there is racism and the numbers are rising.

Comment from the floor I would like to thank the panel up there for sharing. Your story would be no different from my story of the 'Paddy' of the 1950s who went to England and suffered a collection of your experiences. There is one factor that I am very much aware of at this conference and that is the fact that the word 'community' is being used. But I believe community starts with one individual. That is because of my experience in the UK. 'The England of the Welcomes' in the 1950s would not have been known then but there was an England of the Welcomes in the sense that I met an individual there who had the capacity to love the unlovable. And that word 'love' is very much misunderstood as it would have been very much misunderstood by myself back then. There are nine ingredients to it and I am not going to throw them out now. But I will give you a few of them. I think if we understood them and reflected on them more I don't think there would be such a word as 'racism' in any country. One is Kindness, one is Generosity and the other one, which is a very important one, is Guilelessness. I have come to learn and understand those words. I think if we could do that or practice that a little more frequently we would be much better people, no matter what country we were from.

Comment from the floor First I would like to comment on what the gentleman said about other cultures possibly being racist toward the Irish. I believe an ethnic minority can only take so much with the Irish being resentful. I don't feel that ethnic minorities are racist necessarily against Irish people but I feel that if they are constantly being put down and constantly being judged by their colour or their ethnic background they are going to become resentful and diversity and integration are going to become harder to achieve. My point would be that the government is opening its arms to immigrants, yet once they get here there is not enough support. Does the panel feel that they are being pulled into a trap where there is not enough economic support from the government? Do they feel there is a need for a wake-up call to the Fianna Fáil government at the moment?

Katherine As I said, the Chinese community is slightly different. We don't have refugees in Ireland. We set up the first free information service to all the Chinese without any grant, any support. But Irish people from lots of organisations are very supportive and this helps us survive. I would hope that the government would do more.

Adam There is a fair bit of support from the government for the Polish people. If you want to fill up the form for the PPS number, you can get it in English, Irish and Polish. The banks are helpful enough as well; they have brochures in Polish; internal banking and everything is there as well in our own native language.

Katherine You are lucky!

Salome I would say that the government is aware of what I have heard here today. We have submitted papers and we have held meetings with some of the politicians. The one thing they have done is made a commitment with the National Action Plan against Racism, a commitment to work on racism and issues affecting migrants and especially migrant workers. So they know of these issues but I think again it is breaking that culture of silence. It is about speaking out and people not getting offended when looking for solutions to how we can work for a better Ireland. That is the only way we can work things out.

Nilton Ireland has opened the door for anyone to come if you have any skills. Today for Brazilians to come, we do have to apply for a permit first or can wait on a working visa. There is, I think, a lack of support on that. Those people who will come here to work, they will need support, they will need a place to go and talk in their language and get directions for everything. I am not expecting to have support in every single language but I do think that the government has to look more at every nationality and see where the need is and where they can help more. One other thing, I can see in this country that there is construction everywhere. Probably many people know about the health and safety stuff. There are lots of people who are on health and safety courses given in English and they do not understand what is going on. They stay there for a day and do not really understand – what's the point in that? Many people are putting their own lives at risk because they do not understand the rules about safety. The government should look after that.

Cian We are going to finish up with a question from Katherine and, because time is against us, I'll have to ask that anybody who wants to give an answer to meet her afterwards.

Katherine You are a great audience, asking so many questions. Can I ask a question of the Irish people? Why does so much of your money go to charity, to Africa, India and everywhere? Why don't you leave that charity money in your own country to do something for integration, for multi-culture, multi-race? This is a question for the audience.

Envisioning
a New
Ireland

The Price of the Freedom Agenda

David Quinn

Sometimes an idea becomes so familiar that it suffers the terrible fate of becoming a cliché. When this fate befalls an idea, minds begin to switch off. 'We've heard it all before' is the attitude. One idea that has long since become a cliché, or rather is a story that has become a cliché, is the one that describes how Ireland has been transformed from a highly traditional and conformist society into one that is much freer, more liberal, more open-minded, more tolerant.

The story tends to be told in black and white terms. For liberals it is a progression from darkness into light. For conservatives it is often the other way around, that is, a regression from light into darkness. Actually, in a sense, both points of view are right, for reasons I'll explain in more detail later.

For now, suffice it to say that if personal freedom is a primary value for you, then the changes that have taken place in Irish society will seem overwhelmingly positive in the main. On the other hand, if you think having shared values are more important, and that the community is more important than the individual, then many of the changes will seem harmful. Again for reasons I'll try to explain, this is an overly simplistic presentation of these two points of view. For example, can you not believe in personal freedom and in shared values? Can you not find a balance between the individual and the community? For now, however, I want to tell the story of how Ireland has changed in my own way, and in truth, my own way isn't so different from the usual way. I'm going to start in 1922, the year of Irish independence.

In the decades following independence the influence of the Catholic Church in Ireland was massive. Politically, Ireland was not a totalitarian state, but in a way it was a totalitarian society, in that almost the whole of society was striving to create the perfect Catholic community and those who did not wish to go along with this tended to get pushed out of the way. There was an understandable explanation for this desire; the people of Ireland had come to strongly identify, rightly or wrongly, with the Catholic Church in the previous century in particular. It helped them materially and spiritually. It also enabled them to resist British attempts to absorb Ireland culturally as well as politically. Because of this close identification between the Church and people, it was only natural that Ireland wanted the laws of the land to reflect the teachings of the Church, and to this end wanted politicians and bishops to work closely together. Becoming so strongly Catholic was, in part, Ireland's way of saying to the British, you tried to conquer us. You failed. You tried to destroy our distinct and separate culture. You failed. You tried to steal our identity. You failed. I think one reason for the recent decline of Catholicism in Ireland is that we now no longer feel the need to assert our independence from Britain by clinging so tightly to the Catholic Church. In much contemporary writing, the influence of the Church in the past is presented as a kind of imposition on the Irish people. Certainly some people experienced it this way, but the majority did not, although some would argue that this made them doubly oppressed, in that they were oppressed but could not recognise the fact.

The reason the Church was powerful in the decades following independence is because the people wanted it to be powerful. Its power came from the people, and when the people wanted it to be less powerful, it became less powerful. What I am saying is that the influence of the Catholic Church back then was an expression of the democratic will and anything but an imposition on an unwilling people. If you want proof of this then I refer you to the massive Mass attendance in those days. It was over 90 per cent every week and remained so well into the 1970s. I mentioned just now how those who were not willing to help in the building up of a Catholic society were often marginalised. This was the experience of many members of the artistic community at the time, although the extent of this can be exaggerated. Nonetheless, this feeling of marginalisation was experienced by many artists who condemned Irish Catholicism as ignorant, anti-intellectual and emotionally and sexually oppressive.

This brings me neatly on to a theme of many Irish plays and books, the aforementioned sexual repression. Under the influence of thinkers such as Sigmund Freud whose impact on intellectuals in the early decades of the last century was immense, writers, etc. began to explore the subconscious in their works. They often concluded that if emotions and sexuality were not given free expression, up to a point at any rate, the result could only be psychological damage. This was thought to express itself in rage, or joylessness, or neurosis, as well as an eagerness to ensure that no one else was enjoying themselves. And there were people who fitted into this category. They often had willing allies in priests and nuns who saw themselves as a kind of moral police force. Emotional and sexual repression was sometimes allied to repressive and authoritarian behaviour in families. In Irish plays, books and so on we are often presented with the tyrannical father, the repressed, downtrodden wife and the terrified children who are looking forward to the day when they can escape from home.

The Ireland I have just described is largely gone today. There is little of it left. But before I leave it, I want to say a few words in its defence, because it can be defended, up to a point at any rate. Old Ireland, if I can call it that, was certainly traditional. But what is a tradition? It is a way of doing things that has evolved over time and in the heat of experience and has been shown to work. That is why people are reluctant to give up their traditions. They might not be perfect, but they have proven better than the alternatives.

Marriage is an example. Over the centuries, and from culture to culture, marriage has shown itself to be the sturdiest family form, the one that has served its members best on average. Marriages are never perfect, and some are hellish, but if marriage didn't generally serve us well, it would have died out a long time ago. The reason it tends to serve us best is because it offers the best guarantee of bringing together a mother and father in the joint task of raising their children. It is based on the sound idea that children, in general, do better when both their mother and their father are actively involved in their upbringing. So societies should not be condemned simply because they are traditional. As I say, traditions are traditions precisely because they have proven their worth. They give stability and order and cohesion to people's lives. They create community. Most people lived reasonably contentedly within these limits, but happy and contented people don't seem to be as interesting to writers as unhappy people, therefore they don't turn up much in Irish dramas, etc.

If many of Ireland's traditions have been cast aside in recent years it is because some of them at least have served their purpose. The society in which they evolved has changed and therefore the traditions must change or be cast aside altogether. What is filling the vacuum? There is much talk about how Ireland is becoming more Protestant. If this is happening, then it is not registering very much with the Protestant Churches, including the Anglican Church. They are barely holding their own because such growth as they are experiencing is coming mainly through migration. In Ireland there is a very limited understanding of what is meant by Protestantism. To most Irish intellectuals it means the private exercise of conscience in matters of religion and morality. Many Protestants would be insulted by this limited definition and would prefer to focus on Protestant tenets such as 'scripture alone' and 'faith alone'.

Insofar as Ireland is becoming less Catholic, and it is, Ireland is becoming more secular and more liberal, not more Protestant. Against this it must be recorded that very large numbers of people still flock to the holy places of Ireland. The austere retreat island of Lough Derg was in decline for a while but seems now to be attracting more pilgrims again. The shrine to the Virgin Mary at Knock attracts hundreds of thousands of visitors each year. During its nine-day annual novena, about 200,000 people visit it with 70,000 coming for the Feast of the Assumption in August. In 2002 it attracted 1.5 million visitors in all, including many from overseas. The next most visited place in Ireland was the Guinness hopstore with 600,000 visitors. So if you want to stereotype Ireland, there's the evidence. The most popular place in Ireland involves religion, and the second most popular place involves drink. In addition, some 30,000 make the annual climb of Croagh Patrick. On top of all this, five years ago approximately a million people turned out over a four-week period to view the relics of St Therese of Lisieux.

Some Catholics draw comfort from these figures. However, there is a natural religiosity in the Irish people and one wonders if it is that religiosity as much as their Catholic faith which continues to draw pilgrims to the holy places. This thesis is borne out to some extent by the fact that books about Celtic spirituality are extremely popular. One of the best selling books in Ireland in recent years was *Anam Cara*, which is about Celtic spirituality. Some of these books bring the reader back to the spirituality of the early Christian monks, to those who illustrated the Book of Kells, but many go back much further than that to the time before St Patrick arrived in Ireland. Also, Celtic spirituality is often really the New Age, Irish style. It has an almost pantheistic view of nature and rejects the Christian view of sex as repressive.

I asked what is filling the vacuum left behind by the decline of Catholicism and traditional values in Ireland. Is it nationalism? The answer has to be 'no'. It is true that that main standard bearer of nationalism today, Sinn Fein, has seen an increase in popularity. Within the next ten years it could well form part of a coalition government. It is also true that it has no difficulty recruiting members. But it is unlikely ever to become a mass party, and nationalism simply does not capture the imagination of most people, young people especially, today. For them, the national question, namely our independence, has been settled both politically and psychologically. By psychologically, I mean that they do not feel as though they live in Britain's shadow. As for the North, they are content to see it become part of a united Ireland in its own time and certainly don't think it worth dying for.

If both of the two great forces of Irish history – Catholicism and nationalism – have lost most of their power to motivate, and this is even truer of Catholicism than it is of nationalism, then what has taken their place? Irish people, like their West European counterparts, now live in a largely post-ideological, post-Christian age. Indeed, in some ways it is a post-political age as well, because politics also fails to excite. Instead people are turning their energies towards the private life, which is to say they are becoming more individualistic. If I had to name the single most dominant characteristic of Irish life today, I would have to say that it is individualism. Here I get to the heart of my talk. Individualism has gone hand in hand with the rise of liberalism which has advanced under the banner of personal freedom. The great liberal principle is that you should be allowed to do whatever you please so long as you don't do harm to others. In other words, you should be allowed to pursue whatever lifestyle choice you want within this limit. If that choice is to cohabit with someone outside of marriage, then fine. If it is to raise a child on your own, then fine. If it is to be openly gay, then fine. If you wish to divorce, fine. The same applies if you want to have an abortion, although of course you have to go to England for that.

Tolerance is probably the most celebrated and cherished value in Ireland today. The only way people can feel free to pursue their own lifestyle choices is if everyone else tolerates those choices. Live and let live is the order of the day. Is there a price to be paid for personal freedom? I would suggest that there is, just as there is a price to be paid when societies are more traditional and emphasise the community over the individual. The first and most important thing to be said is that sometimes freedom means not simply freedom of expression, or freedom to seek fulfillment in your own way without outside interference. Both of these freedoms are intrinsically good, in and of themselves. But sometimes, and in practice, we define freedom as freedom from responsibility, which is obviously not so good.

Let's consider the realm of sexual relationships. Here the freedom agenda has arguably had its most dramatic effect. Once, you had sex outside marriage at your peril. You risked being ostracised from society if you were caught out. This fell most heavily on pregnant women, but adultery by either males or females could be punished by social exile. Some of the old sexual restraints have rightly been relaxed. However, I would argue here that sex has now been frequently separated from responsibility in the name of personal freedom. The emerging new sexual ethic has two main rules. The first goes like this: anything goes between consenting adults. The second: wear a condom. The first rule tells us we shouldn't care about what sexual acts people engage in. We should only care that the acts are consensual and between adults because obviously if they are not consensual, then someone's personal freedom is being violated. The second rule exists to prevent unwanted pregnancy and the spread of AIDS and other sexually transmitted diseases. But even if we accept, for the sake of the argument, that both of these rules are good in themselves, we must still ask, are they enough? I would suggest they are not. I suggest that these rules on their own are contrary to true human fulfillment. Sex has three aspects, three purposes. One is pleasure. A second is to create feelings of intimacy that encourage us to bond with, to commit to, another person. A third is, some day and in most cases, to produce children. Most of us have, to a greater or lesser extent, a desire to bond with one person, and a desire to have children. These desires are part and parcel of human nature. What happens if these two purposes of sex are suppressed? I think the answer to this is increasingly obvious. We have a growing number of people who expected more from their sexual partners than what turned out to be a commitment-free relationship. Or if they did not expect more, people can find that they have reached their late thirties or early forties and have not found a (hopefully) life-long partner because they passed up on earlier chances to commit. That is, in the name of personal freedom, out of a desire to be unencumbered, they would not commit, and now that they wish to commit, they cannot find anyone to commit to, or who wishes to commit to them.

We also have a growing number of people who, arriving in their late thirties and without children and/or a life-long commitment to someone, find they cannot have children now that they wish it, or that another one of the great desires of most of us cannot be fulfilled. Again, in the name of personal freedom, out of a desire to be unencumbered, they put off having children only to find they cannot have children at all. This applies equally to both sexes. Either that or when they do have a child the other parent refuses to commit either to their partner or the child, again in the name of personal freedom.

In the past, we were often taught that sex was somehow shameful and that we probably should not enjoy it. Today we rightly condemn that attitude as repressive. However, we are now engaged in a new form of sexual repression and do not even recognise it. Sex, whether we are prepared to acknowledge it or not, invites us towards commitment, commitment both to our sexual partner and to any consequent children. However, we suppress this because we want to be free. If we suppress this desire to commit for too long, the results can be emotionally devastating. This is surely one, potentially very high price of the freedom agenda. Clearly we need a new sexual ethic that has a full and realistic view of sex and that recognises all the purposes of sex. Probably we need to evolve towards an ethic of no sex outside commitment. Any true and good sex education programme for schools must teach about sex in all of these dimensions.

I have just dealt briefly with how the desire to be free can conflict with our desire to commit. I now want to deal with another possible conflict, namely the way in which our desire to be free can conflict with our desire to believe in something greater than ourselves. Part of the freedom agenda was dedicated to freeing us from an obligation to belong to belief systems we had no real desire to belong to. This was laudable in so far as it went. However, in order to free us from these belief systems it encouraged in us a sometimes corrosive scepticism that taught us to doubt practically everything. We were led to doubt that there is any meaning and purpose to life at all. We were also led to believe that truth is whatever you want or think it to be. At one level, this is ultimate freedom. It is the freedom to mould the truth to your own liking, to make God, as it were, in your image, not you in his image. But if truth is relative, then there is no such thing as objective truth, that is, a truth that exists outside us, and is waiting to be found.

Having been encouraged to find the truth for themselves, having at the same time been encouraged to doubt there is any such thing as 'the Truth', some people simply never find a belief system that gives them a sense of meaning and purpose. And yet our desire to find a sense of meaning and purpose in life is probably as strong as our sex drive, perhaps even stronger. For example, a lack of a sense of meaning and purpose can drive many people to despair and consequently to drug or alcohol abuse, to depression, and in extreme cases, even to suicide.

It is no coincidence that as what you might call 'ontological scepticism', or scepticism about the Truth, has grown in Ireland, so have problems like substance abuse and depression. If we are suppressing aspects of our sexuality without even knowing it, we are also suppressing our desire for meaning and purpose. Either that or we find meaning and purpose in the wrong things. One of these things is surely consumerism. It is said we live in a post-modern society. In traditional societies we constructed our sense of ourselves and our place in the world out of family, community and religion. Often, of course, that sense of purpose was simply forced on us, or given to us without any questioning on our part.

At the risk of labouring the point, we have weakened all three of these things in the name of freedom, but we still need to construct a sense of identity for ourselves, because the desire to do so is such a fundamental part of our natures. Failure to do this often drives people to seek professional help, sometimes from priests, but increasingly from the therapy industry.

Some sociologists suggest we now construct our identities from what are called 'presentation activities'. That is, we present ourselves to the world, and then ask the world to judge us. If the world admires us, then we admire ourselves, If not, then we are in trouble. Of course, to some extent it has always been so, but as other sources of identity vanish, presentation activities become more and more important. This, the sociologists say, explains the rise and rise of the consumer society. One sociologist describes how the consumer society has changed. He says: 'Shopping appears to have undergone re-skilling from a management task defined by the shopper's ability to select bargains ... to a creative task defined by the shopper's ability to locate unusual, unstandardised, or personalised good.'[1]

In other words, we have gone from being a nation of bargain-hunters to a nation of status-symbol hunters. We construct our identity out of the things we buy. That is, we define ourselves by the things we buy. The things we buy present a certain image of ourselves to the world, and then through the eyes of the world we judge whether we are a success or a failure. For example, am I living in the right kind of house? Am I driving the right sort of car? Am I wearing the right kind of clothes? Among the most popular programmes today are precisely those that tell us what kind of house to buy and how to kit it out, what kind of car to drive, what kind of clothes to wear. These are like the spiritual renewal courses of our day. These tell us how to be fulfilled. 'Trinny and Susannah Undress', a fashion programme airing on UTV, takes this to extremes. Trinny and Susannah, the fashion equivalent of the Redemptorist preachers of old, tell you that they will improve your self-esteem, improve your marriage, improve your sex life, improve your career prospects through telling you what clothes to wear. They offer redemption through fashion. Amend your old ways. Be Born Again.

There is a curious and ironic aspect to this. We like to think we no longer live in a judgemental society. In fact, we are as judgemental as ever. Instead of making moral judgements, we are more likely to make what you might call 'social status judgements'. Are you a 'winner' or a 'loser', socially speaking? Note how the word 'loser' is now used so commonly. It has replaced the word 'sinner'. You are no longer a moral failure, you are a social failure. In the name of freedom we demolished the old belief systems. But we still need something to believe in. That is the way we are made. For many people consumerism has filled the void. But consumerism encourages us to see ourselves through the eyes of others more than ever, making us more dependent than ever on the good opinion of society. No one cares anymore whether you are living with someone before marriage, but they do care about the sort of home you live in, the car you drive, the clothes you wear. Get these things wrong, and prepare for the opprobrium of your peers. In other words, and in a certain way, many of us are less free, not more. However, it has to be said that being subject to the judgement of society is not always and everywhere a bad thing in itself. What would be the prospect of us morally improving ourselves if we did not sometimes subject ourselves to the scrutiny of others, if we were not willing to see ourselves through their eyes? I am thinking here particularly of our loved ones.

The question remains, what are we holding up to judgement? In the past we were judged according to certain moral criteria, mainly Christian ones. We wanted to appear to society as good Christians. This could lead to deeds of genuine altruism. It could also lead to hypocrisy and false piety. Today, we show our virture by being tolerant, which is actually a very undemanding virtue. The person who is selfish in every other way could also be extremely liberal in his or her social attitudes. But with regard to consumerism, when we hold up an image to the world based on what we buy, perhaps there is little room for hypocrisy, but there is plenty for superficiality. So I say again, sometimes it is good to have to be judged by society. The trick is to hold up the right kind of traits for judgement and then somehow to avoid becoming censorious. This is not easy. Nothing good ever is. But society can act as a constraint on some of the worst kinds of behaviour and can be a source of moral improvement. In the name of personal freedom we should not entirely discount this function of society.

Emile Durkheim, who conducted the first proper study of suicide, found that those least likely to commit suicide were those who lived within boundaries, which is to say, the boundaries, or constraints, formed by our belief systems and by our relationships. A recent book, well worth reading, is *The Happiness Hypothesis* by Jonathan Haidt (2005), Associate Professor of Psychology at the University of Virginia. It should be said at the outset that Haidt describes himself as a liberal Democrat atheist. Despite this, however, he is mainly well disposed towards religion. The reason for this is as follows. His book uses scientific research to try and discover what is most likely and least likely to make people happy. He discovers that there is more wisdom in religious thinking than is commonly supposed today.

For example, at one point he compares two people. One is the very model of the successful modern man. He is healthy, well off, with a high status career. He is youngish, single and has no children. He is the essence of the unencumbered self, as outwardly free as anyone could be. The second person is a woman in her sixties, a church-goer suffering from ill-health who lives near the poverty line. She is involved in a variety of communal and voluntary activities. I won't give you any prizes for guessing which of these two people Haidt says is more likely to be happy. It is the woman who by all standards of worldly success is a failure, the person who has taken on commitments. The point Haidt makes is that all the evidence shows that the happiest people are likely to be those who have taken on commitments, who live with boundaries, who accept limits to their freedom.

Of course, this also brings us on to the corrosive effects of the freedom agenda on our sense of community. But this is a well worn path, so there is no need here to go into it in depth. Suffice it to say here that people are disengaged not only from the Churches. They are disengaging from politics and from social volunteerism. It is striking that fewer and fewer people turn out to vote at election time. It is also true that fewer and fewer people are joining political parties, let alone putting themselves forward to run for office. You might say that politics is suffering from its own vocations crisis, just as the Churches are.

As in other western countries, it is mainly older people who vote. Voter turnout is particularly low among young people, just as church attendance is. All of this is indicative of a crisis of commitment. It is also reflected in Ireland's growing divorce and separation figures. If we are suffering a crisis of commitment, then one casualty has to be marriage, which is one of the greatest commitments of all. Children are also a very big commitment of course. We often hear of children rebelling against their parents. But parents often rebel against their children and can often give up on the demanding task of parenting even while living in the same house as their children. What are we to do? We need to refine the freedom ethic. We need to develop a much better theory of happiness. Let's remember that all this hard-won freedom is aimed at making us happier. We need to learn that a reluctance to make commitments out of fear of sacrificing our freedom and independence increases, not decreases, our chances of finding happiness, on average. However, these commitments cannot be forced on us. They must be voluntarily undertaken. The mistake of traditional societies is to force many commitments on us, which we can then experience as a terrible burden. The mistake of modern, liberal societies, however, is to sometimes think freedom is enough. Against this, to counter this, we must be encouraged to voluntarily take on commitments, and then we must be given good reasons to stick to them. The biggest reason, needless to say, is when children are involved. Children, as I say, can be very big casualties of the freedom agenda.

In terms of educating people about the purpose of commitment in our lives, I suggest that *The Happiness Hypothesis* is a good place to start. The book is written for a popular audience, but allowing for that, it is a sort of social manifesto. It might also have been called *Reforming the Freedom Agenda*. I believe that all societies are faced with a choice, and the choice involves a trade-off between different values. A traditional society will have relatively little personal freedom but will have plenty of social cohesion. There will be a strong sense of community and meaning. A liberal society prefers personal freedom and the price is a loss in social cohesion, a loss of that sense of community, a growing sense of meaninglessness. You cannot automatically say which of these two types of society is better. It really depends on what you value most. If you like personal freedom, then you will approve of many of the changes that have taken place in Irish society. If you prefer tradition, community, social cohesion, then you might not. Personally, I like a blend of both, but so far few societies, or at least not in the English-speaking world, seem to have found this blend. The challenge for us is to find it. We can find it by convincing people that they will not be less fulfilled if they give up some of their freedom to take on commitments, or to follow a given belief system, they will be more fulfilled. If we can do this, then I believe we will have achieved real progress.

Note

1   Taken from G. Reekie, 'Changes in the Adamless Eden: The Spatial and Sexual Transformation of a Brisbane Department Store 1930–1990, in R. Shields (ed.) *Lifestyle Shopping*, London: Routledge, 1992, pp. 170–94.

Wasting Time with People

Alice Leahy

The topic of 'Freedom: Licence or Liberty?' is so apt at a time when many of us are asking fundamental questions about the world and a rapidly changing Ireland. We seem to be wondering how we can make this a truly inclusive society. Indeed, despite all the dramatic change we have witnessed, it is disturbing how undervalued human contact and genuine caring for others has become. We may be rid of the work houses, the orphanages and even the psychiatric hospitals, but, as one senior civil servant said to me recently, this leaves prison as the last refuge for many of those vulnerable and unable to cope, whose difficulties are criminalised simply because there is no where else to send them. You will appreciate with that brief introduction why I am very happy to speak about 'wasting time with people'!

I grew up under the shadow of Slievenamon in South Tipperary, part of a small family in a close-knit community. Everyday we thought of our aunts and uncles forced to go abroad to seek work in the UK, US, Australia and New Zealand – some of whom choose the religious life. Memories abound: cycling miles to see Tipp and Cork play in the Munster Final; my grandfather forecasting the weather from the colours and shadows on Slievenamon; my grandmother singing, 'I dreamt I dwelt in marble halls ' as she crocheted. Work, reading, drama, debates, environment awareness projects, recycling, picking fruit and veg for country markets (of which my mother is the sole remaining founding member of the first branch in Ireland) visiting old and sick neighbours, some in the county home, ensured I was a very active citizen and was aware of the value of social capital before the term was coined. My adopted home of Dublin introduced me to the slums, especially while working as a midwife in the Rotunda. All of this sowed the seeds of what I do now in a dramatically changed Ireland.

One of the most important things we make for those we see every day in TRUST is time, time to treat people as human beings. This is the one thing that is increasingly difficult in the modern Ireland where we all seem to be statistics, reduced to a quantitative or monetary value. In a world increasingly governed by performance indicators and benchmarks, based on these quantitative measures is it possible to preserve even the concept of a philosophy of inclusivity, which means fundamentally treating people as people and as equals? The focus on people is being lost even as more resources are being deployed because it becomes almost impossible to advocate for a philosophy of inclusivity and caring when we distance ourselves from people. This distance is aided by technology: voicemails, emails and a flawed consultative process – all seemingly designed to keep people at a distance. But how can we ensure that people are treated as people? This is the most basic human right – the right to be treated as a human being and not a statistic, as the award winning South African satirist Pieter Dirk-Uys so eloquently put it to me when I met him some years back. Another African voice was quoted not too long ago in an article in the British Medical Journal. Simon Challand, a medical adviser working in Uganda, relayed some advice an African Bishop had given him with a smile:

> 'Waste time with people … You Europeans are always concerned about projects and budgets. The African does not worry about them – just waste time with people.' He gave me this advice in 1996 shortly before I came out to work in Uganda. Since then his

> words have kept coming back to me, and I reflect on
> their truth and wisdom and how difficult it has been
> for me, as someone with European values and
> attitudes, to apply them.

However, what those so far removed from the frontline in the development and planning of our health, social and homeless services fail to understand is that you cannot really listen to people without taking time to do so. Time is much more productive in the long term because by listening to people today they will not become isolated, disillusioned or be made to feel worthless. Listening to people means we can help them avoid the misery of despair and exclusion in a 'democratic' society.

Let me describe our daily work in TRUST, an organisation founded in 1975 which grew out of research I carried out in night shelters with a group of doctors working in a voluntary capacity. That work, and the generosity of the late Ann Rush, led to the foundation of this private, charitable trust. Our aims are:

> to serve homeless people in need by promoting
> human services which would meet their immediate
> and long term needs and by these means to
> encourage their development and give their lives a
> dignity which is their birthright.

The service we set up was the first of its type, and has been used as a model for services here and overseas. We are sandwiched between St Patrick's Cathedral and Christ Church Cathedral in the Liberties area of Dublin. We work in the basement of the Iveagh Hostel and are grateful to the Iveagh Trust who only charge us a nominal rent. The philosophy of TRUST is based on two central principles:

- The recognition of every individual's right to be treated as an autonomous and unique human being.
- The need to restore the dignity of individuals whom society has labelled deviant and undesirable.

Every day we meet over fifty men and women who sleep rough and welcome others as they present themselves to us – all outsiders in a city of plenty. Many come from outside the city, some from the remotest parts of Ireland, some returning to the land of their birth to be buried in the 'old sod' and many from outside the jurisdiction, with increasing numbers from the EU Accession States. Some we have grown older with, meeting them first in the early 1970s. Of course we meet new people every day. We employ two nurses and provide a medical service, advice and dressings; sometimes it looks like a casualty ward as many people we work with will not go to A&E, and even if they do they often will not wait. As part of a holistic service we provide bath and shower facilities, a complete set of clothes and information on rights and entitlements. We seek to treat people as people, recognising that they need help and have rights, especially their right to privacy. In coming to TRUST we hope people feel secure and trust us. Hospitality is important – we provide tea and coffee as we would to welcome visitors into our own home.

The people we meet are perceived by the wider society as being different and difficult. They suffer from the effects of isolation, neglect and health problems, exacerbated by what are often described as chaotic lifestyles. Accessing mainstream services – particularly basic accommodation – is a major problem. We increasingly meet people who were 're-settled' in totally unsuitable accommodation, and then find themselves homeless again. I meet people homeless in Dublin whose heartbeat I listened to while working as a midwife in the Rotunda and consider it a sad reflection on our society that we are now meeting second and third generation homeless. These people present with a wide range of medical problems. These include bodies ravaged by disease and violence; some with pressure sores from sleeping out in all weather, sometimes sleeping in urine-soaked clothes for weeks; infected and untreated minor skin conditions and major skin problems such as leg ulcers and gangrene, lice-infected heads and scabies. In addition, we often meet people who are suffering from malnutrition and all of the medical conditions common to the general public but exacerbated by their living conditions. We still treat conditions long disappeared since the advent of good food e.g. trench foot and impetigo (wild fire) – conditions clearly linked with extreme poverty.

Some people we meet cope with very serious addiction problems, including drugs, alcohol and gambling, and suffer the despair and the pain of loneliness. These people are pushed from service to service, often unable to get relief for minds at breaking point, with the only solution a brown envelope of medication with directions that make no sense. Many people we meet struggle to create a sense of normality after years locked away in institutions, and others who have been relocated from one institution to another. And some who are locked in prisons they have created for themselves, often out of the frustration of not being understood or ignored. Of course, as Bob Dylan once said, 'we are all prisoners in the mystery of the world'. Many people we know have attempted suicide, and many have died on the streets. We meet some people who are so cut off from everything around them that they at times appear to be beyond reach. Others, however, challenge and inspire us everyday to look at the way we live our lives.

People coming from the EU Accession States are not all coping well – like some of our own people who went to England and America out of necessity in the past. Piotr, a Polish man in his forties, arrived in Ireland almost two years ago. He lived in a hostel for a few months and got a job, which he later lost. He never got the money owed to him so he could not pay for a hostel bed. He had poor English. He has an eighteen-year-old son and an eleven-year-old daughter. He phoned them last on Children's Day in Poland. It costs money to phone. Going home to Poland isn't an option; there is no work for him there and he likes Ireland. I met Piotr on the day of the Dublin–Mayo match. He was excited as he set off to watch it in a shop window. When he arrived in on the following Monday I asked him what he thought of the match and he said, 'You crazy football', to which I replied, 'you should see the hurling'!

Sometimes the only hearing these people ever receive is when they are being researched. This is an issue we have grave reservations about because of the quality and quantity of research taking place today, as well as the time and money spent on 'evaluating outcomes and cost effectiveness' while ultimately making no difference to the lives of those researched. Some people who are homeless, poor, or just different feel pressurised to take part in research into homelessness in case they lose their hostel bed or their entitlements. We only become involved in research when we believe the research design is sound, ethical and likely to provide useful information, and we would be concerned about the sharing and storage of confidential information without due regard for the rights of our fellow human beings. 'Tracking People' has become a much-abused phrase and is currently seen as best practice. Tracking people through the system smacks of Big Brother as more and more vulnerable people are forced to trade personal information to get a very basic service. The most recent 'common assessment tool' based on one designed outside our jurisdiction will be 'rolled out' shortly – a huge intrusive document where data will be computer stored and, I guess, shared. This is of great concern to me and my colleagues.

This is of course fundamentally about human rights in the sense of respecting people as people and refusing to see them as mere statistics to be measured and researched like inanimate objects. Undoubtedly research is essential to plan services.

> If we are to push for fundamental change in the whole area of homelessness, then a certain amount of constructive research is necessary. We feel strongly, however, that it must be pursued with the greatest caution. It is clear to us that the 'research industry' uses that section of our society, which is the most vulnerable and the least able to battle for

its rights as its source of material. We must never forget that we are working with human beings, who for the most part have been battered by our society and who for so long have been pushed about as just another number in a cold inhuman bureaucracy.

This quote from Leahy and Magee from 'Report on Broad Medical Services for Single Homeless People in the City of Dublin' was compiled and produced on 7 March 1976. Now, thirty years later, in a new millennium, what has changed? Our frontline service providing care to the most disadvantaged people in Dublin over a long period has given us some unique insights into the way in which the services, voluntary and statutory, operate in Ireland and beyond, and of course we all view the world from where we stand.

To be without a home is to be suspect. The homeless are easy targets. Their bodily integrity is constantly at risk. Their lives are an offence against the sacred canons of private property and consumerism. Their privacy is regularly intruded on as part of the price of being statistics in the poverty industry; their painful experiences are reduced to sociological research data. The true test of a civilised community is how people at the margins are treated. Not only must individual liberties be defended, but society should be educated and sensitised towards a broader vision of life and living.

Dan Sullivan, then President of the Irish Council for Civil Liberties, writing in *Not Just a Bed for the Night* (Alice Leahy and Anne Dempsey, 1995), describing what it means to be homeless in Ireland. That compelling piece is as valid today in a new century. The unchanging nature of life for the outsider in Irish society also inspired us to launch 'Building Trust in the Community', an initiative to build on the work we have sought to do in recent years to change attitudes and encourage more people to become advocates for the outsider.

Until those in positions of power and influence are prepared to sit with people in their misery and poverty, feel their pain, smell the smell of misery and waste, feel the trembling body and listen to the cries of frustration and at times consider challenging ideas or words of wisdom, rather than looking at statistics in neat boxes with grandiose titles, nothing will change. They should not allow jargon to take over and should be prepared to question rather than using reports to further distance themselves from people, or just support entrenched ideas they may already have. If they can not or will not do that a growing number will continue to suffer pain, often the pain of not being listened to, and those of us meeting with them are left with the feeling that we are only adding to their misery through our silence. Indeed, many people, including those in Church, State and Community groups who work hard in building and fostering community involvement, are also beginning to feel disenfranchised by an increasingly insensitive bureaucracy and meaningless jargon.

In July this year a bulletin sent to the staff of the HSE by email from 'internal comms' included a job description for the newly created position of Head of Process and Operations. It stated that this will 'involve executive leadership of cross-pillar operational and process change, sponsorship of process developing projects and the cascading of process excellence throughout the HSE'. This was later quoted in the letters page of *The Irish Times*, 24 July 2006. I shall repeat this and just ask if you know what it means? Can such an appointee, if such a person exists, understand what I am saying or, more importantly, even understand those charged with the responsibility of dealing 'hands on' with people.

A widening gap is developing between the bureaucrats and those in front line care. Those who suffer most through the refusal or inability of those running the services to listen and 'waste time with people' are the most vulnerable – the very people the services were set up to help, such as Joe.

Joe has been known to us for twenty years. He came from rural Ireland and was born a few months after the Easter Rising, turning ninety this month. He worked all his life, paid his way in a workman's hostel in Dublin after years in the UK. He remained single; he walked miles until quite recently when 'the pains' curtailed his independence. He never longed to go back to the mid-western area he came from as he preferred city life. He liked to visit the local pub, have a chat, watch the races (the smoking ban put a limit on perhaps his only social encounters outside the hostel where he lived.) He dressed well, keeping his only suit hanging in the wardrobe and his shoes polished. He wanted to live his life independently for as long as he could. As the twinkle in his eye dulled and the pains altered his gait, making him almost completely bent over, he ultimately decided to move to a nursing home some months ago. He had promised me he would let us know when he felt he should and we promised to help him. I shudder to think how he would have coped alone with the process of negotiating with a cold, insensitive and often very incompetent bureaucracy, as the following will illustrate.

A bed became available in the place where some former residents of the hostel he called home had settled. We knew it as a warm, caring environment where the matron and a voluntary committee ensured the best quality care was provided in a friendly setting. He visited the place, was assessed by the medical personnel and was accepted. To enable his transfer some procedures were required, including subvention. This process could be fast-tracked we were assured, as his health continued to fail and our concerns increased. Geraldine McAuliffe, Deputy Director of TRUST, my colleague, worked constantly for three weeks without success to secure nursing home subvention. She described the experience as soul destroying. The endless calls that went unanswered and the messages that were not passed on serve to underline just how bad things have become and why those who have no one to speak up for them have absolutely no hope.

A bed for the man was secured but the nursing home could not let him have it until the subvention was sanctioned by the HSE. Following several phone calls to the relevant staff and being left holding, listening for long periods to an interminable jingle, Geraldine eventually secured a commitment. However, it was subject to the condition that the man was examined and confirmed as suitable by a geriatrician, which would take months as there is a long waiting list to obtain such an examination. This required many more calls until the HSE conceded that he could be examined by a Public Health Nurse. However, when the local PHN was contacted, she insisted he had to be examined by the Public Health Nurse attached to his GP's practice. The PHN in the practice agreed to do it on the last day before she went on holidays if the forms could be faxed to her and asked if he qualified for subvention. After hours on the phone Geraldine secured a commitment that the forms would be urgently faxed to the practise. When she checked, assuming everything had gone according to plan, she discovered that the fax arrived four days late! In the meantime, because of the delay in securing the subvention, the bed in the nursing home had to be given to someone else. This means that Joe has spent the last six weeks in an acute hospital bed. Therefore, when you hear about bed shortages in our hospitals, in many instances it is due to an excessive zeal on the part of those running the services in seeking to ensure that regulations are enforced to the letter, regardless of the human cost which is unquantifiable. However, you will also hopefully appreciate that if there was more humane concern for the plight of this vulnerable elderly man, the HSE would have freed up an acute bed and allowed him to find some sense of home in the nursing home where many of his friends from the hostel were also cared for. It is clear that the training of personnel requires much more than just filling in forms. Freedom, liberty and indeed choice should be basic rights in a wealthy transforming Ireland! However, as Joe's experience illustrates, things are getting worse rather than better for the most vulnerable in some situations.

Tom who looks seventy but is only in his mid-fifties lives in Dublin 4. One day a week, before 8 a.m. he makes his way to TRUST, along Patrick Kavanagh's well-worn path on Baggot Street, Stephen's Green and Grafton Street. He carries a large ESB golf umbrella, which he got in TRUST, and holds all of his earthly possessions in a small plastic bag. He likes this time of year: the dark evenings mean he can go to bed early – his home is under the bushes in a park. Recently a Welfare Officer decided that his money, a meagre €165 a week (try living on it) should be stopped because he refused to move into a hostel. The Welfare Officer told me it was a ministerial order and that was that! This highlights, in quite compelling terms, why people with no voice rely so much on anyone they can find to intercede on their behalf with the bureaucracy. TDs and senators and local public representatives, as well as local groups in the community who should not have to play a role in softening the impact of an apparently heartless system all come into contact with a system often more interested in enforcing the letter of the law rather than making certain that the rights of the citizen to a service are made easy to obtain. In that regard anyone who listens even occasionally to the *Joe Duffy Show* will understand what I am talking about and the vital importance the media plays in informing people of their rights and protecting them.

Legislation too can impact on the lives of people who should be able to relax in the autumn of their lives. How many, for example, are aware that VAT is charged on care in the community. Many do not have the freedom to live out their days in their own homes. Indeed, many live in fear in their own homes because of crime, breakdown of neighbourhood values and the closure of rural Garda stations. Some facilities for people are not available countrywide, like access to free travel and free chiropody for the elderly, to mention just two – both of which would help people to enjoy freedom of movement and access to social activities. Many older people experience real poverty because they feel they must save money for their funeral rather than enjoy a little luxury. The impact of the closure of some rural post offices, rather like the closure of small hospitals in Dublin, has never been properly assessed. Often services put in place can further isolate and label people rather than enhance the enormous value of socialisation.

We must be acutely aware of the social determinants of health and be prepared to discuss them and stop intimidating those who speak out, forcing them to remain silent and conform. Mary Robinson, former President of our country, said in 2001, 'Each time you speak out with a critical voice you pay a price'. On the other hand, if we are honest, we don't encourage people to speak out as the lack of proper whistle blower legislation, especially in the health and social services, clearly shows. Caring for people as citizens does require us to speak out if we feel people are being denied care and liberty. If anyone is not being treated with dignity or, worse still, being excluded from society or our world we have a big responsibility to be their voice. We also need to care for each other and defend those who speak out or nothing will change. Care to my mind is about concern, about defending a person's most basic right and we should be careful when using words like 'caring community' unless we respect everyone's rights, as the mark of a truly caring society is one that respects everyone in equal measure. I reflect often on the words of Pastor Martin Niemoellen in 1945:

> First they came for the Communists, but I was not a Communist so I did not speak out. Then they came for the Socialists and Trade Unionists. I was neither so I did not speak out. Then they came for the Jews, but I was not a Jew so I did not speak out and when they came for me there was no one left to speak for me.

A Christmas morning a few years ago I happened to catch Eurovision Mass from Circus Pinter Top in Paris. Apart from the charm and artistry of the Parisians I was struck by a few quotes from the Pastor: 'Encounters with people move us.' I am sure our isolation in offices at times does something to us too and he further said: 'It is the blind application of the law which makes us inhuman.' I suggest that much of what is presented we accept blindly and perhaps knowing the cost of speaking out we remain silent. Of course that silence helps to build the walls that make outsiders of the most vulnerable and also those brave enough to speak out. Why? As a society we profess we are committed to human rights and guaranteeing everyone's rights is supposed to be important. However, as I can see everyday with the people I work for, their rights are not respected and on a day-to-day basis, as I have already described, they are humiliated and must endure the almost casual denial of their human rights. We do not describe the poor treatment of the voiceless and the most vulnerable in our society as human rights abuses. Of course, we use words and phrases like 'denying their human dignity' and rarely even mention their rights. Somehow their disgraceful treatment is not serious enough to be considered as a denial of human rights. However, Article 1 of the Universal Declaration of Human Rights states that 'all human beings are born free and equal in dignity and rights'. From what I have described today, I hope you will appreciate that many of the people I meet everyday are victims of human rights abuses, though many would not dream of suggesting such is even possible in Ireland, so blinded have they become by the propaganda and PR spinning emanating from the insensitive bureaucracy with such awesome power over their lives. However, by looking at the conditions and the way in which those who are marginalized in our society – from those who are homeless on the street to elderly people unable to care for themselves – and by questioning whether their human rights are being protected and respected, we can bring about radical change.

For thirty years TRUST has been involved in advocacy work – trying to be a voice for the voiceless – as well as providing health and social services. Today, through the development of human rights based approaches, which can be developed into a potential management philosophy in the health, social and homeless services, we have the potential to transform the way the most vulnerable are treated. However, it is vital that everyone becomes involved and it is not seen as a legalistic formula of how to deal with people but as the right way to treat people and each other. The example given of the official stopping a vulnerable homeless man's disability cheque without any sense of his rights in that situation is a classic example of how and why human rights education must be extended to all officials in the services. It should not be seen as just an exclusively legal or academic exercise. If we want a caring and respectful bureaucracy managing our health, social and homeless services, one that places respect for the dignity of every individual at the very centre of its operations, we now know that by adopting human rights based management approaches we can achieve this.

Some years ago in the Royal College of Surgeons in Ireland I met Phil Barker, former Professor of Psychiatric Nursing, who runs workshops on the premise that 'knowledge can only be gained through experience'. I once wrote to him for permission to use a quote and he replied: 'Alice, people don't remember what you say or what you do. They will remember how you made them feel.' This excellent advice comes to mind daily. Oscar Wilde also said something that is probably more true of today's Ireland as our values have become much more materialistic: 'We know the price of everything and the value of nothing.' Only by 'wasting time with people' will society ensure there are no outsiders and that all can participate fully in the transformation of what is increasingly seen by many as a State losing its way.

Time is priceless and in our rush to develop services or copy other nations we find it increasingly difficult to accept this fact. Because of this inability we miss out on the values that make for good citizenship and inclusivity. In our rush to be seen as a great nation are we forgetting that we are an island race with a long, chequered history, a treasured culture and huge talent? We should now have the confidence to reflect on some of the wisdom from the past from rural and urban communities – not confining the debate to academic circles and visiting experts – and we should not be afraid to pose awkward questions. As John Boorman, the acclaimed 73-year-old film director, whose film *The Tiger's Tail* raised interesting points, said in a newspaper interview, 'the dynamics and prosperity are invigorating', though he was rightly concerned about the 'social and emotional consequences'.

Everyone in their own way needs to consider where they stand and what kind of community they want. The power to change things is in our hands.

Knowledge is Freedom, Freedom is Knowledge

John Quinn

I am sure you are wondering about the title of this paper. So am I! Originally entitled 'Knowing your place, Knowing your place', the organisers thought that this might look like a misprint. Today I wish to speak about the concept of knowing ourselves, where and how we fit into this world – the ultimate goal of education. When I talk of knowledge, I am not talking of factual information that will help you do well in the pub quiz or, dare I say it, in much of our exam system. One of the old problems with education is the confusion of schooling with learning – that nothing is learned unless it is taught. Learning transcends schooling.

If I were to ask each of you to recall an outstanding learning experience, what variety we would hear in your answers? How many of them took place in school or through a book, film, radio interview, mentor, apprentice, travel, mistake. This is not to denigrate school – it forms a critical and crucial part of our education, but when it is reckoned that schooling only accounts for 20 per cent of a young person's life, we must ask what fills and influences the other 80 per cent? Further, that 20 per cent is still heavily influenced by an industrial society that required basic skills and the ability to follow orders and be cogs in a machine, an industrial society that no longer exists. Today's society demands curiosity, initiative, collaboration, adaptability from our school leavers. Contrast that with the annual analysis of the Leaving Cert in the media – the angst and the paranoia over what came up, what should have come up, what didn't come up, what came up that *never* came up before. What comes up is *life*, with all it delights, disappointments, cruelties, vicissitudes. There was a feature in *The Irish Times* recently on a girl who attained 600 points. She stated that there was 'no point in knowing stuff that's not going to come up in exams. I learned the formula and practised it endlessly. I was always frustrated by teachers who would say, "you don't need to know this for the exams but ...".'[1] And she is studying to be? An actuary. There is nothing personal in my remarks. She is a product of the measurement culture, which decrees that only that which can be measured, assessed, tested is of value – a by-product of which is the hideous notion of school league tables. It is a culture that makes our exam system a national version of *The Weakest Link,* that pays little or no heed to the notion of Howard Gardner's Multiple Intelligences and equally pays little heed to the words of Albert Einstein: 'Not everything that is countable counts. Not everything that counts is countable.'

Mike Cooley, who addressed this conference a couple of years ago,[2] elaborates on this when he speaks of the tacit knowledge he observed in people when he was growing up in Tuam – the blacksmith, the dressmakers. If I may quote from his *My Education* interview:

> Tacit knowledge was explained by the philosopher of science, Polanyi, who said that there are things we know but cannot tell. It is a sense we have of shape, size, form and appropriateness which we acquire through practice, through relating to materials, to working with materials. Since it cannot be written down or explicitly stated, there is a tendency for modern educational systems to ignore it or say that it doesn't exist, that the only important things are those things which we can state explicitly. I saw vivid examples of this during my childhood. There was a stonecutter in the town who made a gravestone for

our family and I remember him saying to me, 'If you come back next week the head will be coming out of the stone', as though it had been born from the stone. He was really like Michelangelo: he could already see the figure in the material and all he had to do was remove all that which was not the figure.

I remember going to Galway when they still used to make the Claddagh shawls. It was an astonishing piece of textile design, in the best sense of the word. I have seen people get degrees in fine art at the Royal College of Art in London who, in my view, couldn't even begin to approach those kinds of skills, although they could write about them – so I became conscious very early on that our society values linguistic ability more than real intelligence and that is something I have tried to address throughout my lifetime.[3]

Beyond the walls of school, beyond the chains of certification, beyond the prison of professionalism there is an awful lot of tacit knowledge. One of the wisest men I knew was Johnny Kelly, a bog man who never went past primary school, but who knew his trade of turf cutting and the love and legend of his native place – knew his place. Closer to home, Marie Murray, who addressed Céifin last year, wrote movingly in her *Irish Times* column about an amazing Clare woman who died a couple of years ago – Sr Eucharia Keane. Again, if I may quote:

This woman who spent a lifetime counselling and empowering, working with adolescents, giving cookery classes in her home, botany lessons to children on the nearby Burren, knitting for new babies, providing post-natal encouragement to mothers and marital support to couples, consolation for those bereaved, encouragement to the depressed, practical visits to her friends in the Travelling Community, meals to school children who were hungry and hospitality to all who entered the ever open door of her home, would no longer be permitted to dispense such largess into other people's lives today. This is because she had little formal teacher training, no social worker qualifications, diplomas in psychogeriatrics, career guidance training, post-grads in social injustice, psychology degrees, prisoner rights diplomas, social care certificates nor was she accredited as a child, adolescent, adult or marital therapist.

What was once called neighbourliness has become 'social capital'. Family supporters require registration. Words of common sense and wisdom are copyrighted intellectual property and doing a good turn has legal and insurance implications.

But she once worked in a night shelter in London, with 'down and outs' in Leeds, with families in Fatima Mansions in Dublin and in a home for ex-prisoners in Ballyfermot. She was a founder of Clare Care and lived for twenty years in Corofin providing a best practice model of community endeavour, local empowerment, spiritual support and invitation to the transcendent.[4]

What an extraordinary part Sr Eucharia played in so many people's lives! There is a saying: It takes a village to raise a child. But what has happened the village and where is the child? Here is Jim Deeny, born one hundred years ago, recalling his childhood in Lurgan, Co. Armagh:

My father and mother and my sister, brother and I lived next door to my grandfather, my grandmother, two aunts and an uncle. We were a bit like a commune. In addition, we were reared with a governess, a remarkable woman, Miss Finnegan. We would walk along the street with her and stop to look at a shop window. Twenty yards further on Miss Finnegan would ask, 'And what did you see in that shop window?' We would tell her as many things as we could remember and then she would take us back again to see how many things we had missed! We also had a big farmyard and paddocks right in the middle of the town and there were a couple of men working there. They all took care of us and minded us.

My other grandfather lived up at Dungiven. He was a contractor, a farmer and a mill-owner. One of my uncles ran the contracting business. He was also the local head of the St Vincent de Paul Society. As he went from one building to another, some old lady in a pony and trap might meet him and he would have a wee chat with her about getting help from the St Vincent de Paul Society. In this way I learned from him. The grandfather took me for a walk every Sunday. Because he was a builder, he could tell me all about the ruins at Dungiven or he would take me up to Poll na Péiste, The Dragon's Pool, which is now flooded for the waterworks for Derry.

I used to run wild through the countryside. I had friends like the canal lock-keeper, who built me a boat for two pounds and I used sail it on the canal. Then there was Herbie Andrews, who was head of the waterworks. He showed me how to run the waterworks, which valves to turn, what to do when the filter beds got clogged. And Hughie McAlinden took me fishing in his boat.

I used to be sent to get shoes soled at Lavery's the shoemakers. I would sit there for half the morning talking about shoemaking. Then Mr Lavery would go to feed his pigs and I would help him and forget to come home. I really was a dreadful child! I had a wonderful childhood, running wild one minute and then strapped down and taught to play the piano ...[5]

Truly it took a village to raise him, a whole community. But 'Ah', you say, 'that was one hundred years ago – when there *was* community, time and no technology. Now we have little community, *no* time and *all* the technology.' But Sr Eucharia only died a year or two ago. Was she a one-off? Why should she be? Yes – community is under siege. The people are still there, more and more of them at an older age, a whole army of retired people with talent, wisdom, experience and *time*. Mary Surlis showed us last year how she is tapping into this with her wonderfully innovative *Living Scenes* – older people sharing learning in the classroom and outside it. It can be done! I have seen it done and it is so right and natural and productive and beautiful. I would love to see a nationwide SOS – Sharing our Skills – where tacit knowledge is *freely* shared in a community. It would be a way of rebuilding, refocusing community.

Mentor was the experienced and trusted advisor to Telemachus, son of Ulysses in Homer's *Odyssey*. Young people need mentors. Here's a marvellous account of mentoring from John McGahern, taken from his *My Education* interview:

There were no books in our house, but I discovered them in the house of friends of my father, a family called Moroney. There is a wonderful portrait of them in that good book *Woodbrook*, by David Thompson. Old Mr Moroney was a beekeeper and he was very eccentric. Father and son lived together and they had 180 acres of good limestone land. In fact, David Thompson says they were landless, but in a way they were landless in spirit. They had a farm that they never looked after and in fact they gathered apples and sold them for half a crown a bucketful. I remember being sent to buy a bucketful of apples and falling into conversation with the old man about books. I was interested in books and when I was about eleven he gave me the run of his excellent nineteenth-century library. For about eight or nine years, I would come every fortnight, returning five or six books in my oil-cloth shopping bag and taking five or six more away.

I imagine the Moroneys had once been ruled by women, but at this stage the two boys were on their own. They would run through all the cups and plates and every month they used to have a big washing up. They lived on tea and bread and jam. Willie Moroney was a great beekeeper and he had an enormous beard which was stained with all sorts of colours of food and drink – you could smell him at quite a distance. When he was talking about books and the raspberry jam on his bread fell into his beard, it set off a buzzing noise. Without interrupting his conversation, he extracted three or four bees from his beard, cast them off into the yard and went on with his conversation. His son was interested in astronomy and so they did practically no work on the land at all. He was also interested in unusual breeds of sheep. I remember going with him in a van with five or six special sheep that they had imported from England to sell at the Dublin market. He wanted to see the stars, so we went out to the top of the Sugar Loaf mountain and were absolutely frozen sleeping in the van. We sold the sheep in the morning and had breakfast in the big hotel at the cattle market. They were both lovely people, so gentle.[6]

What an education! The *real* point is how much do we as a society owe to the Moroneys? Would we have a writer like John McGahern in whose home 'there were no books'. Surely we are indebted to the Moroneys, eccentrics, oddbods, cranks, outsiders but full of tacit knowledge and wonderful mentors. Ah, I hear you say – that was *then*. This is *now*, unrelenting, busy, busy, pressurised *now*. We don't have the *time*. We are caught up in the Religion of Rush, as John O'Donohue calls it:

> We have lost our capacity to engage creatively with time. Rather than being subjects of time, we are its victims.[7]

Is it a modern phenomenon? Consider these lines:

> Life is eating us up
> We shall be fables presently
> Keep cool!
> It will all be one a hundred years hence.

They were written a century and a half ago by Ralph Waldo Emerson. A century and a half later life continues to eat us up, but at an even more frightening pace. From the cradle, the child is rushed through the sluice gates of education. Even before the cradle, training the child *in utero* is now in fashion. The fastest growing educational software is for children aged 6–24 months. On and on, through the sluice. Be competitive. Get ahead. Get a grind. Know the system. Get the points. Through the sluice gates of examination, where some get through (and not undamaged) and some don't because they are the weakest links. And then what? Why didn't we give them time? Time to meander, as Penelope Leach puts it. Time to stop and stare, to pause and ponder, to do *nothing*.

Here's Sean O'Faolain – again one hundred years ago – on his Auntie Nan's farm in Co. Limerick:

I did nothing. I sat by a well and saw a spider race with delicate legs across the cold water from out of his cavern. I saw a line of cows pass along a road, their udders dripping into the dust. I went with Uncle Tom, each of us seated on a shaft of the donkey cart jolting out to his bits of fields in the Commons near Lough Doohyle, taking with us for the day a bottle of cold tea and great slices of wheel cakes cooked in a bastable, plastered with country butter and cheap jam. While, all day, he went slowly up and down the ridges on one knee thinning his turnips, I wandered. I saw a row of twenty poplars whispering to the wind. I picked and chewed the seeds of the pink mallow. I saw how the branch of a thorn tree in the armpit of the alder had worn itself and its lover smooth from squeakingly rubbing against it for forty years. I saw an old ruined castle and a Big House with the iron gates hanging crookedly from its carved pillars. And all the time away across the saucer of the lake there was the distant church spire of Rathkeale, like a finger of silence rising from an absolutely level horizon.

You see? Nothing! A fairy tale, a child's memory, a cradle song, crumbs in a pocket, dust, a seed. I lay on my back among lone fields and wondered whether the cloudy sky was moving or stopped. Childhood, boyhood, nostalgia, tears. Things no traveller would notice or want to notice but things from which a boy of this region would never get free, things wrapping cataracts of love about his eyes, knotting tendrils of love about his heart.[8]

A blessed and glorious nothing that was everything in terms of learning.

Children are biological beings, not machines. They need time to grow and develop, time to reflect, play, interact. Instead we hurry them. As they grow older, the pace increases when in fact they need the 'gift of the interval', as Michael Oakeshott puts it. Young people need to acquire the habit of reflection because they won't pick up that habit in later life. Rather, in middle age there will be a sense of opportunities lost, of dis-ease. We need to take a long hard look at what we are doing to children and childhood. Penelope Leach was one of 110 signatories of a recent open letter to the *Daily Telegraph* calling on the British government and public to understand the realities of child development. Children, they say, need life to be *real*. They need real food, real play and real adults – not junk food, sedentary screen-based entertainment and absent adults. They need *time* and protection from stress. This is not a plea for nostalgia, a return to idyllic days of Jim Deeny, Sean O'Faolain or to school through the fields. Of course there was poverty, ill-health and physical hardship – not to mention the darkness of abuse – in those times. But there were also, as Marie Murray has pointed out, 'freedoms, mental space, time, structure, opportunities to be close to animals and nature, to use the imagination and to learn to cope with adversity'.[9]

In his book *Last Child in the Woods – Saving our Children from Nature Deficit Disorder* (2005), Richard Louv laments the modern child's distance from nature. 'In the space of a century,' he argues, 'the American experience of nature has gone from direct utilitarianism to romantic attachment to electronic detachment … Today's core belief is that nature is in the past.' Paradoxically, today's children probably know more about the Amazon or the Antarctic than they do about the plants or birds in their own neighbourhoods. What they are missing, Louv argues, is the tactile, random experience that is central to child development and mental health:

> For a new generation, nature is more abstraction than reality … something to watch, to consume, to

wear – to ignore. A recent television ad depicts a four-wheel drive SUV racing along a breathtakingly beautiful mountain stream – while in the back seat two children watch a movie on a flip-down video screen.

The resulting 'nature deficit disorder' in both children and adults has produced what Louv calls 'cultural autism' characterised by 'tunnelled senses, and feelings of isolation and containment. Experience, including physical risk, is narrowing to about the size of a cathode ray tube or flat panel ...'

How many street or park games do you see children play today? Sometime you should read *All In! All In!* (1984), Eilis Brady's marvellous collection of children's games and rhymes.

We played simply for joy. We were never bored and the games cost nothing. A piece of rope attached to a lamp post or strung between two gate posts and you could swing away to your heart's delight. Boys lifted the lid of the water-hydrant and it became the mowl into which they pitched buttons or coins. A piece of chalk and an empty shoe-polish tin were all you needed for 'beds' or hopscotch. Just hopping up and down steps became the basis for another game. We used our environment ...

Adults didn't pay (or didn't need to pay) the slightest attention to children's games. This was the only time children were totally without adult supervision. We made our own rules. There were no prizes – just the joy of waiting your chance and maybe occasionally winning a game. When you were 'out', that was it. You accepted that and waited your chance again ...[10]

Of course, it's a Paradise Lost. Eilis Brady acknowledges that, but we can learn from it, we can adapt. Why *have* we no time for children to play, to meander? The philosopher Rousseau famously said, 'Do not save time but lose it'. Why have we no time for *ourselves*? Who dictates this? Why can't we slow down? Why? Why can't we *be*? We are after all human *beings*.

Of course the problem today is not 'to be or not to be', but 'to have or not to have'. Rather than being an inquisitive society we are becoming an acquisitive society. No longer, 'I think therefore I am' – now it's 'I *have* therefore I am' and 'I will *have* more therefore I will *be* more'. Our culture (our advertisers?) tells us there is no limit to what we can have. Anything can be bought. In his book *The Secrets of Happiness* (2006), Richard Schoch says:

> Unhappy is the story of happiness. More than two thousand years ago, when the ancient Greeks first thought about what constitutes 'the good life', happiness was a civic virtue that demanded a lifetime's cultivation. Now, it's everybody's birthright: swallow a pill, get happy; do yoga, find your bliss; hire a life coach, regain your self-esteem. We have lost contact with the old and rich traditions of happiness, and we have lost the ability to understand their essentially moral nature. Deaf to the wisdom of the ages, we deny ourselves the chance of finding a happiness that is meaningful. We settle, nowadays, for a much weaker, much thinner, happiness: mere enjoyment of pleasure, mere avoidance of pain and suffering ... Somewhere between Plato and Prozac, happiness stopped being a lofty achievement and became an entitlement, happiness as entitlement.

How many more spas do we need? And yet are we happy? According to Henri Nouwen, one way to express the spiritual crisis of our time is to say that most of us have an address but cannot be found there. There seems to be a mountain of obstacles preventing people from being where they want to be. 'If I were to wish for anything,' says the philosopher Kirkegaard, 'I would not wish for wealth or power but for the passionate sense of what can be.'[11] The Chinese put it more simply: happiness is having something to do, something to hope for, someone to love. Each one of us has that 'can be' within us. Each of us has that possibility.

Ben Zander has written a wonderful book, *The Art of Possibility* (2000). He is conductor of the Boston Philharmonic Orchestra and a professor of the New England Conservatory of Music. As a teacher, he has developed with his wife Rosamund the practice of giving an 'A'. At the beginning of the academic year he informs his students that each one of them will get an A for their course of studies. There is one requirement that the students must fulfil to earn that grade: 'Sometime during the next two weeks, you must write me a letter dated next May, which begins with the words, "Dear Mr. Zander, I got my A because ...".' The student must place themselves in the future, looking back on all the insights and milestones they attained during the year. Everything must be written in the past tense. Ben Zander is interested in the person that each student will have become, in their attitudes, feelings and world view. Each must 'fall passionately in love' with the person described in that letter.

Zander draws inspiration from Michelangelo's concept that inside each block of stone or marble there dwells a beautiful statue:

> If we were to apply this visionary concept to education it would be pointless to compare one child to another. Instead, all the energy would be focused on chipping away at the stone, getting rid of whatever is in the way of each child's developing skills, mastery and self-expression.[12]

For the teacher this innovative approach 'transports your relationships from the world of measurement into the universe of possibility.'

Giving an A can be applied in any relationship or any walk of life. It is not restricted to an elite of gifted students of music. The A is not an expectation to live up to, but a possibility to live into.

> I dwell in Possibility –
> A fairer House than Prose –
> More numerous of Windows –
> Superior –
> for Doors –[13]

It is a very subtle but wonderfully liberating approach. Zander invites his students to dream. How many of us have been censured for daydreaming (or worse, have censured others)? Tony Buzan has said, 'If you don't daydream you die'.[14] Yet all the dreamer does is to give slack to the imagination – imagination, which our friend Einstein reminds us, is far more important than knowledge. As John O'Donohue writes:

> A human life can have everything – beauty, status, reputation, achievement, all kinds of possessions – but if the imagination is not awakened, all these lack presence and depth.[15]

Kornei Chukovsky, the great Russian observer of language development in children, has remarked: 'The present belongs to the sober, the cautious, the routine-prone, but the future belongs to those who do not rein in their imagination.'[16] We are essentially that which is greatest within us, and our aim should be to live up to that greater self. Too often in education, in life, we fear or are made fear that greater self when, as the writer Marianne Williamson reminds us, we should be celebrating it:

> Our deepest fear is not that we are inadequate. Our deepest fear is that we are powerful beyond measure. It is our light, not our darkness, that most frightens us. We ask ourselves who am I to be brilliant,

gorgeous, talented, fabulous? Actually, who are you
not to be? You are a child of God. Your playing small
does not serve the world. There is nothing
enlightened about shrinking so that other people
won't feel insecure around you. We are all meant to
shine as children do. We were born to make manifest
the glory of God that is within us. It's not just in some
of us: it is in everyone. And as we let our own light
shine, we unconsciously give other people permission
to do the same. As we are liberated from our own fear,
our presence automatically liberates others.[17]

How well does our formal schooling serve the Imagination? 'Must
try harder' is probably the answer. W.B. Yeats once famously said,
'Men have set up a great mill called Examinations to destroy the
Imagination'. Our schooling, dictated by examinations, is heavily
left-brain oriented, the logical, linear, cause and effect – is there a
book on it? what's the *answer*? – to the exclusion of the right brain
– what if? supposing that ... how did *that* happen? We are besotted
with seeking 'the right answer' when often there is no right answer.

The American poet Carl Sandburg writes:

> The white man drew a small circle in the sand and
> told the red man, 'This is what the Indian knows,'
> and drawing a big circle around the small one, 'this
> is what the white man knows.' The Indian took the
> stick and swept an immense ring around both circles:
> 'This is where the white man and the red man know
> nothing.[18]

There is a whole lot more to reality than we can ever know. So to
get back to reality, much of what I have been saying may seem
unreasonable but as G.B. Shaw once remarked, 'All change comes
from unreasonable men [and women]'. John Abbott, who also
addressed Céifin some years ago, says in relation to formal
schooling:

> We need people who are competent problem-solvers, creative, flexible and personally responsible for their welfare and the welfare of those in their family and neighbourhood. [19]

To achieve that we must take into account modern research in the way we learn – what Abbott calls going with 'the grain of the brain'; the role of technology in independent learning; the recognition that adolescents are capable of taking responsibility for much of their own learning – with tutoring rather than 'teaching' from adults; the recognition of multiple intelligences; the possibilities of intergenerational learning; of learning beyond the walls of the classroom; and that education is a lifelong process.

Now that – we are told – the points race is over (due to expansion of courses, decline in school leavers) – there will be opportunities for real innovation in curriculum and the organisation of learning. Professor Tom Collins, Head of Education at NUI Maynooth (another Céifin graduate) has recently posed that challenge:

> A more fundamental approach would aim to change the child's experience of second-level education away from subject-specific coaching to one which is developmental in focus and exploratory and investigative in methodology. It would be more holistic in approach, drawing upon the multiple intelligences of the child and emphasising the importance of social and emotional well-being, self-motivation and capability for self-directed learning. It would shift the teaching role from one which relies primarily on instruction to one which is focused mainly on enabling and facilitating learning.[20]

Charles Handy has also posed the challenge in his book *The Elephant and the Flea*:

> If I were in charge of our schools, I would be tempted to divide the day in half, one half to be spent in the classroom acquiring knowledge and the skills of analysis – the other half outside, on projects and activities that would cultivate process skills and experiences. We might need a different set of teachers for each, but the process skills could well be taught by volunteers from the community, through apprenticeships or through attachments to ongoing projects.[21]

You may say, isn't that what Transition Year or projects like the Young Social Innovators do? Yes, but they are only tinkering with the process. They need to expand beyond a particular year, to be properly organised and overseen and ultimately recognised through continuous assessment. Why shouldn't a Leaving Cert student get recognition and credit for work as a teaching assistant with infant classes, for research on 'Addiction in our Community' or for putting on a drama in a nursing home?

We need to foster curiosity and collaboration in our young people and a spirit of inquiry and possibility. We need to open the doors of our schools for a two-way flow of traffic – elders, mentors, volunteers inwards and students outwards into the community, not at the same time, of course. We need to slow down, to give ourselves and our children time. To quote John McGahern in his last book, *Memoir*:

> The best of life is lived quietly, where nothing happens but our calm journey through the day, where change is imperceptible and the precious life is everything.[22]

Is it all a dream? An impossible dream? It need not be. We can make individual choices. I will conclude with a response from two of our greatest poets:

Seamus Heaney from 'Station Island':

> Let go, let fly, forget
> You've listened long enough
> Now strike your note ... [23]

And finally the words of Louis MacNeice from 'Autumn Journal':

> If it is something feasible, obtainable
> Let us dream it now
> And pray for a possible land
> Where the altars of sheer power
> And mere profit
> Have fallen to disuse
> Where nobody sees the use
> Of buying money and blood
> At the cost of blood and money
> Where the individual, no longer squandered
> In self-assertion, works with the rest.[24]

Let us dream it now. Let us work for it now. Let us be unreasonable.

Notes

1 *The Irish Times*, 20 September 2005.
2 *Imagining the Future*, Céifin Conference 2004.
3 *My Education* (ed. by John Quinn) Dublin: Townhouse, 1997.
4 *The Irish Times*, 5 September 2005.
5 *My Education*, ibid.
6 *My Education*, ibid.
7 *The Sunday Tribune*, 25 December 2005.
8 *Vive Moi! An Autobiography*, London: Rupert Hart-Davis, 1965.
9 *The Irish Times*, 16 September 2006.
10 *The Open Mind*, RTÉ Radio, 2000.
11 From Ben Zander, *The Art of Possibility*, Harvard: Harvard Business School Press, 2000.
12 *The Art of Possibility*, ibid.
13 Emily Dickinson, *The Poems of Emily Dickinson*, Harvard: The Belknap Press of Harvard University Press, 1951.
14 *The Open Mind*, RTÉ Radio, 2001.
15 *Working towards Balance*, Céifin Conference 1999.
16 *The Child from Two to Five*, Berkeley: University of California Press, 1963.
17 *A Return to Love: Reflections on the Principles of a Course in Miracles*, New York: HarperCollins, 1992.
18 'Circles' from L.B. Hopkins, *Hand in Hand: An American History Through Poetry*, New York: Simon & Schuster, 1994.
19 *The Unfinished Revolution*, Stafford: Network Educational Press, 2000.
20 *The Irish Times*, 19 September 2006.
21 London: Hutchinson, 2002.
22 Faber & Faber, 2005.
23 From *Station Island*, Faber & Faber, 1984.
24 From Charles Handy's *The Hungry Spirit*, London: Hutchinson, 1997.

Tax and Community

Frank Daly

This audience, I suspect, is somewhat different to the congregations of tax practitioners, accountants and assorted financial experts who usually have to listen to me. Just to make one point initially. I am giving a personal view today, so while you may certainly take it that this view influences my approach as Chairman of Revenue and as a public servant, I don't wish to put it forward to you as official Revenue – still less government – policy. Please bear in mind also that I am a full-time civil servant and have hopes to remain so for at least another short while!

A Transforming Ireland – A Transforming Revenue

I am very taken with the title of this year's conference and particularly with the concept of 'engaging with a transforming Ireland' because this indeed is a very good description of what Revenue now does every day. Over the past few years we have been transforming ourselves to deal with the new Ireland and the particular challenges this has brought. I like to think we have been responsive and quick to adapt but by no means would I claim that we are perfect or that there is not more we could have done or not more that we can do. There is a wider debate to be had sometime perhaps about the way in which the public service as a whole in this country has involved itself in the transforming Ireland and whether it has been a leader, driver, onlooker or follower – but that's not for today.

A 'transforming Ireland' of course will mean different things to different people and will pose different challenges for different organisations and sectors. For Revenue the challenges have focused around a booming economy, an extraordinary increase in our business (and therefore our workload), managing wealth (from a tax aspect), changing work patterns, the new 'techie' Ireland, a changing workforce and different expectations (often lifestyle influenced) of citizens and our own staff.

For example:

- The number of self-assessed taxpayers increased by 45,000 in 2005 compared to the previous year. In the same period the number of PAYE employments increased by 135,000. These increases are more than maintained to date in 2006 and recent reports talk of over 15,000 new businesses registered in Ireland since last January.
- There is increased complexity in the cases we deal with (more people have shares, investment income, rental income and so on).
- There is a new challenge of dealing with the vibrant multicultural society that Ireland is fast becoming – in practical terms giving extra support to those whose first language is not English and who are not familiar with the Irish tax system.

These factors (and they are only a few examples) mirror exactly Harry Bohan's apt depiction of: '... an economy registering unparalled growth, a rising population buoyed by an enriching emigrant community ...'[1] We in Revenue experience the reality of that description every day because Revenue, what Revenue does and how Revenue does it, connects with and impacts extensively on our economy and our community.

Funding Government

Government funding comes from taxes, and for a long time now! You can go back as far as ancient Rome or start with Pitt's introduction of income tax in 1799 or Gladstones' extension of this to Ireland in 1853 – wherever you start, taxation is now accepted as the means by which government provides for the public good. Tax generates almost all of the finance necessary to provide services, to develop infrastructure, to provide security and so on. It also, in most modern societies, has become a tool through which government seeks to develop the economy, redistribute resources to the less well off and influence behaviour positively, as, for example, with tax incentives to encourage certain types of development or negatively, as for example to wean people away from using plastic bags or smoking. Although it should be unnecessary therefore to say it, taxation is not for the Revenue, it is not even for the government. Ultimately, it is for the people, for the community.

This year over 94 per cent of the resources that the Irish government will spend will come from central tax revenues, duties and levies – the monies gathered by the organisation which I represent. This makes all of us in Revenue very aware of the importance of what we do and acutely aware that what we do is ultimately for the benefit of the community. In fact, without an awareness of that wider dimension, tax collection for me (indeed my job) would be a rather sterile affair. It becomes a totally different matter when I focus on what tax will be used for:

- Perhaps to ease the lot of somebody on social welfare.
- Perhaps to dignify the final days of somebody who is ill and cannot afford private healthcare.
- Perhaps to give a break to some carer by providing respite care for a loved one.
- Perhaps to rehabilitate a prisoner and give him or her another chance.
- To make our communities safer.
- To develop depressed and rundown parts of our country.
- To provide development aid to a struggling nation.
- To encourage inward investment and provide good jobs for more people.
- To help welcome and integrate our new people from abroad.
- To support the individuals and groups who give so much of their time and effort voluntarily in education, sport and other caring initiatives.

I could go on with this list and no doubt you could add to it. Suffice to say that this is what makes the job I do worthwhile and I know it has the same resonance with my colleagues in Revenue. It is no accident that Revenue's Mission Statement begins with the words: 'To serve the Community ... by fairly and efficiently collecting taxes and duties and implementing import and export controls.' I am conscious of course of the additional contribution we make through our customs service to keeping society protected from drugs but that is for another day – our focus here today is on tax.

Influencing the Way We Do Things

The bottom line for Revenue then, indeed our primary business goal, is to collect the taxes and duties that are due and ensure that those who owe them, pay them. This is not just what government requires of us. It is also what the community requires of us so that resources can be deployed and redirected for the benefit of all. It is also what individuals and individual businesses require of us so that they can be assured that they are being treated fairly compared to neighbours, colleagues or competitors. Revenue's whole approach to administering the tax system has been well articulated in recent years – it is a combination of what we call the 'soft' and 'hard' approaches. The 'soft' approach encourages voluntary compliance by working to make it as easy as possible for people to pay their liabilities through quality and accessible services for taxpayers. We have done a lot in that area in recent years with on-line service, information provision and by becoming a more open and approachable organisation. We have more to do and take it from me, we keep working on this every day. The 'hard' approach on the other hand is to provide a sharp and uncompromising response where there is non-compliance. Whether you believe it or not, this is not our favourite activity but it is, unfortunately, a necessity. It comprises activities such as audit, compliance visits, enforcement and, of course, special investigations. As far as I am concerned, it is part of the unwritten contract we have with those taxpayers who pay their share – the deal is that if you pay then we will tackle those who do not.

There has never been a greater commitment or focus on this by Revenue and this focus will continue. Our ideal of course would be to see the need for the 'hard' approach diminish as more and more people pay their share voluntarily – we are making encouraging progress towards this ideal but there is still quite a way to go.

The Legacy of the Past

Whatever about engaging with the present and preparing for the future, the harsh reality is that we are still busy confronting the past. The legacy of widespread institutionalised tax evasion, which came to light in recent years, is deplorable. I will leave to you and others to consider the lost opportunities and think about 'what might have been' if Ireland Inc. had access to the hundreds of millions in revenues that were evaded over a couple of depressed decades. What an opportunity cost indeed!

What have become known as the 'legacy investigations' have been a major work item for Revenue. We have regarded it as a challenge and an opportunity. The challenge lay in how we responded to the revelations. If we were not clearly seen to vigorously pursue these frauds how could we ever look compliant taxpayers in the eye and ask them to continue their voluntarily compliance? The culture of non-compliance would be seen to be rewarded and hopes of promoting a culture of tax compliance in this country set back enormously. The opportunity lay in convincing people, by our response, that Revenue would not tolerate evasion, that time would not diminish our determination to pursue it, that we had the powers, the resources and the will to follow through – that we would keep our part of the deal with compliant taxpayers. I know there have been some who did not fully support Revenue's determination to pursue these legacy cases, arguing that this was all in the past and that we should leave it there; arguing that it was wrong to pursue people now for old debts and liabilities; pointing out that in some cases payment of these liabilities was creating hardship. They argued that it was not fair. As far as Revenue is concerned, however, there could never be the option of walking away from this systemic and widespread evasion – in our view that is what would not have been fair – and in Revenue we are committed to treating all taxpayers fairly. It is the very first commitment we make in our Mission Statement: to serve the community by *fairly* and efficiently collecting taxes and duties and implementing import and export controls.

Fairness – Legacy Investigations

This matter of fairness is interesting and indeed apposite in any discussion on tax and community. Fairness is a fundamental value for us and I would like to talk about it for just a minute, firstly with regard to the legacy investigations and then more generally with regard to the wider tax system.

To those who say that it is unfair to pursue taxpayers who engaged in tax evasion twenty years ago I would say that I understand why the opinion is held but I need to ask these questions: What about fairness for the honest citizen? What about fairness for those who struggled every week to pay their taxes? What about fairness for those who struggled to keep businesses going in the face of unequal competition subsidised by tax evasion? What about fairness for those who may have been deprived of better services because tax revenues were not what they ought to have been during those years? Obviously I have a particular view of the answers.

Most of you will know by now that Revenue has collected over €2.2 billion from these legacy investigations and there is more to come. But I have often emphasized that these investigations were never about money alone – they are about something much more important. These investigations, the revelations behind them, the publicity that attended them and the demonstrated determination of Revenue not to ignore evasion by any sector or individual, have proved to be key drivers in promoting a growing public intolerance of tax evasion and an increasing public awareness of tax obligations. I have no doubt that they have also contributed to some restoration of belief in the fairness of our tax system.

Fairness

By now you may sense that I have a bit of a thing about fairness in the tax system – I certainly hope so! Allow me to talk about it in a broader sense than just the legacy investigations.

For a start my preoccupation with fairness in the tax system is not just because all of 230 years ago Adam Smith listed equity or fairness as the first of his four Canons of Taxation, nor is it that I am any more paranoid than your average Irishmen about paying for the round when it comes to my turn. I am sure some of my preoccupation with fairness comes from the fact that, like most Irish people, I have an inbuilt sense of fairness and fair play. But mainly my preoccupation with fairness in the tax system stems from my role and from a clear belief after forty years in the Revenue service that if our tax system is not fair or perceived to be fair, then our goal of a tax compliant society will never be realised. The ideal as far as I'm concerned is a tax system in Ireland that is resonant with fairness. What does that mean? Do we have it?

A Fair Tax Structure

To answer this we need to deal with two aspects – the basic *structure* (a matter largely for government) and the *administration* of the system (a matter largely for Revenue). Needless to say, as a civil servant I am much more comfortable talking about the latter rather then the former! In discussing structure the debate will inevitably deal with the political policies and choices that determine the shape of our tax system – matters like the relative contribution of direct and indirect tax, whether stamp duty is properly structured, whether we should have more taxes on property, whether we should have more or less local taxation and the like. There will be strong views about the place of tax incentives in a tax system. There will be views that these are likely to be of most benefit to the better off – sometimes conveniently forgetting the considerable benefit for the community at large of the outcomes (we have plenty of examples of these in the modern Ireland). These are essentially political choices – like everybody else in this audience I have strong personal views on these matters but it would certainly be inappropriate for me to comment publicly. I'll leave it to the body politic.

However, leaving aside the individual political choices that shape our tax system, I would expect and am quite prepared to say publicly that a tax structure 'resonant with fairness' would at least contain these fundamentals:

- Be based on classical principles which define a good tax system – equity, simplicity, transparency – treat people largely on the basis of their ability to pay but take equally from those with equal means.
- Require an overall 'tax contribution' that is reasonable and seen to be so. International comparisons will be relevant here as will relative levels of state intervention in different societies – material for another fine debate!
- Be required and used by government for productive, responsible and acceptable purposes – including as a tool of economic and social development.
- Be responsive and adaptable to the elimination of any abuses or unintended inequities as they are identified. Tax is complex and it is unrealistic to expect that any system can be totally immune to abuse or unintended effects – the important point is that these are constantly searched for and promptly eliminated.

Evaluating our present tax system by reference to those fundamentals, I am confident that in Ireland we are in the right space. We can be satisfied, but should not be complacent, about the basic fairness of the structure of our system. In particular I would argue (because it is an area we in Revenue have some responsibility for) that we now have a system that is responsive to searching out and dealing with abuses and to identifying and neutralising unintended effects. One example relates to the unintended effect of the aggregation of reliefs and incentives which enabled small numbers of relatively well off people to either eliminate their tax contribution or reduce it to unacceptable levels. This effect, as revealed in Revenue's series of Top 400 Taxpayer surveys, certainly did little to help the perception of fairness in our tax system. The last Budget sought to deal with this and introduced what is in effect a minimum effective tax rate for high wealth individuals. We should of course remind ourselves – because we cannot be selective in applying our standards of 'fairness' – that not so long ago we needed the impact of those incentives and the money of those investors to help rebuild our economy and get it to the 'booming' stage that is underlying the theme of this conference today.

A Fair Tax Administration?

What then about the administration of the system – is that 'resonant with fairness' today? Well, that is certainly directly in my sphere of responsibility. Some of the fundamentals for fairness here will be:

- That Revenue deals with all taxpayers equally and without fear or favour.
- That we administer the law consistently and reasonably.
- That we treat everybody courteously, in a non-discriminatory way, and that we preserve confidentiality.
- That we make everybody aware of their entitlements, give them every assistance with their tax affairs and expect and encourage them to pay no more than they should.
- That we are an open and accountable organisation.
- That we have open and easily accessible mechanisms for complaint and review.
- That we are relentless in our pursuit of those who do not comply.

Many of you may recognise some of these as ingredients of our Customer Charter. I am sure everybody here will have a view as to how we measure up to these standards. I would hope for a general acceptance that we have the right attitude, the right approach and a strong commitment to these fundamentals of fairness. I would hope for an acceptance that we work hard at delivering what is necessary and that we are getting better at this every day. I certainly assure you that, insofar as we are not yet where we would like to be, it is not down to any lack of will or commitment – but perhaps sometimes the day to day struggle of managing a complex system, a rapidly growing workload and a constantly changing environment means we cannot always go at the pace we would want to. We are encouraged by the results from a recent survey of 2,000 small and medium sized businesses where 68 per cent of respondents agreed that Revenue's approach to administering taxes and duties is fair.[2]

Evasion and Avoidance – The Real Unfairness

Most people I speak to make it very clear that by far the main criterion by which they judge whether our tax administration is fair is by reference to whether people pay what they should. Revenue certainly should be evaluated by reference to the effort we put into this. There are two methods by which people do not pay what they should – tax evasion and tax avoidance. (Obviously there are people who at times may have a genuine inability to pay but that is a different matter.) Tax *evasion* is a black and white affair – it is always inexcusable. We have been very visible in recent years in dealing with it. I have already referred to the legacy investigations, you will be aware of the quarterly publication of tax defaulters, you will have heard of our new focus on prosecuting people for tax evasion and many of you will be aware of targeted projects like those in the construction sector in 2006. So this is an area where we have really upped our game and are getting very good results. Indeed in that recent survey, nearly 70 per cent of respondents agreed that Revenue is effective in dealing with tax evasion.[3] Evasion is not a grey area – it is wrong and it is unfairness personified. A tax system 'resonant with fairness' cannot tolerate it.

But what about tax avoidance? Well if tax evasion is black and white, the mists really descend when tax *avoidance* is mentioned. Yet these days any discussion of fairness in a tax system cannot avoid this subject. It is difficult to define tax avoidance – in layman's terms it entails either manipulation of tax law or exploitation of gaps or unintended consequences to give a benefit which was clearly never intended by the legislature. A single clever avoidance scheme is capable of giving the beneficiary a very significant 'tax gain' – often amounting to a sum that would dwarf the 'gain' in a straightforward tax evasion scam. Avoidance is somewhere on the spectrum between evasion (always wrong) and legitimate tax planning (always right). Some commentators refine the definition a little – acknowledging a difference between so-called 'aggressive' avoidance and (presumably) 'ordinary' avoidance – although I could note with some amusement that antonyms for 'aggressive' include 'friendly' and 'submissive'! Defenders of avoidance put the case that tax is merely a matter of law. They argue that if it is legal then it is ethical and that morality or values don't come into it. To put this argument of course of itself betrays a set of values. As one academic put it:

> It is important to realise that one cannot escape decisions about business values. To take the view that 'business is business' is itself a decision which reflects one's values (in this case – probably – the value that one should maximise one's own personal gain).[4]

Aristotle has argued that justice cannot be entirely contained in legislative measures and that at its best justice is fairness. A French academic commenting on this says that 'someone who is fair is therefore just, even eminently so, *but in the sense that justice is not mere conformity to law but a value and a moral requirement*' (my italics).[5] I believe most people would find it hard to accept the proposition that just because something can be shown (or be artificially structured) to fit within the strict letter of the law that it then doesn't really matter if it clearly offends against the spirit and purpose of the law or against the intention of the legislature. We could of course get into a debate here about 'literal' or 'purposive' interpretation of the law in the Irish courts system but perhaps we should just note in passing the enactment of the Interpretation Act, 2005, which provides for the position that, where a literal interpretation would fail to reflect the 'plain' intention of the legislation, preference will be given to the intention of the Oireachtas, where this can be ascertained from the Act as a whole.

I believe in fact that the majority of people act by reference to principles or standards which are not defined in any Act of the Oireacthas but which are based on values derived from a sense of social and civic responsibility and from the 'norms' of the community of which they are part. Their actions have regard to an unwritten moral code which is influenced by these wider principles at the expense of a principle of just personal gain or advantage. One Australian academic, discussing tax avoidance, put it like this:

> What needs to be fostered is a change of attitude to the law, in which it is seen not as a game of words, a material to be worked on to one's own or one's client's advantage, but as an instrument of legitimate policy to be respected, with the policy, not just the words, looked to as the measure of compliance.[6]

Evasion and avoidance offend the community because of the real sense of unfairness they generate in those who practice neither. They offend also because they subvert the intentions of democratically elected government. Government develops programmes of capital and current spending, including social spending and long term infrastructural development based on expected Exchequer funding largely provided by projected tax revenues. These revenues are based on government and Parliament-approved taxation policies and taxation rates. It is we who elect the government and by doing so we give them the authority to make such decisions – including defining a tax base from which they can reasonably expect to fund their plans and programmes for the common good.

Attitudes to Compliance

Before I finish I would like to address a question that I seem to be asked a lot lately. Is Ireland now a tax compliant country? I think it would be naïve of me to say it is. But I do say with some confidence that we are a more compliant country than ever before and that we are moving in the right direction and at a fair pace. The improvement is partly driven by Revenue's recent initiatives, partly by a growing intolerance of non-compliance and partly by a growing awareness of the function of tax in community.

This is a welcome maturity in our attitudes and we need to foster it. We must keep hammering home the message that tax compliance represents not just a legal obligation but also a civic duty, a central element of social responsibility and a core component of good citizenship. I agree with the former President of the Irish Taxation Institute who referred, quite rightly, to '… the civic duty of all citizens to pay their fair share of taxes'.[7] The old concept of a 'social contract' is very relevant here: citizens enjoy rights such as security, proper legal process, access to education and health services. Business expects that the infrastructure will support its operations and its further development. All these public goods are bought through taxation, and failure to pay our fair contribution is nothing short of depriving ourselves and our fellow citizens of our rights and selling ourselves short on our legitimate expectations.

Over the last quarter of a century or so we have seen attitudinal change in many areas. Drink driving might never have been approved of but it was condoned by many people. Twenty-five years ago someone taking up a job in the civil service was usually shown to a desk with an ashtray on it. That is unimaginable now – it would also be illegal of course. We have also learned to be careful with our language – President Kennedy in the early 1960s promised to 'put a *man* on the moon before the end of the decade'. Today he would probably promise to put an American on the moon. We are careful not to offend – and rightly so. Although I might mention in passing that even the most liberal writers and journalists seem to feel it is perfectly acceptable to refer to an entity called the 'Tax Man' – a phrase that is both sexist and pejorative at the same time! I think it is fair to say that attitudes to tax compliance have mirrored these changes. Tax evasion, and increasingly even aggressive tax avoidance have joined drink driving, smoking in public offices, sexist language and insurance fraud as once tolerated but no longer acceptable to the vast majority of people.

Fostering this New Maturity

The compliance effect of Revenue's own activities will of itself never get us to the stage where we can say we are truly a tax compliant society. We need to build on the attitudinal maturity. We can do a lot more in the field of educating people and explaining to people what exactly is the role and function of taxation in society and convincing them of the very direct connection between taxation and the common good. We have lots of debates in this country about taxation but they almost always focus on the 'burden' of taxation (and, as an aside, wouldn't it help if we began to use the term 'tax contribution' rather than 'tax burden'?), or on the components of the tax system or the latest scam or the performance (or non-performance) of Revenue and of course it is not surprising that most of them revolve around different political ideologies.

We need to broaden the focus of the debate to address the role and function of tax and we need to get a wider audience involved – the taxation debate should not remain the remit of politicians, academics, tax practitioners or indeed Revenue. I would like to see the role of taxation feature more in our early schooling curriculum

143

– building perhaps on the existing Civic, Social and Political Education Syllabus (CSPE) at junior level and into our transition year programmes at senior level. I would like to see the role of taxation on the radar of community and voluntary groups, of trade unions, of summer schools and of conferences such as this. Most Sundays I hear thoughtful and stimulating homilies in church but it's quite a while since I heard one about the role of taxation in community! Certainly Revenue would be more than willing to assist in these areas in any way we can – short perhaps of giving Sunday homilies!

Conclusion

Tax is not merely a business cost, not merely a drag on business and the individual. It is the contribution which we all make towards the common good – it is how public services, infrastructure, security, economic policy and even government itself are funded. In simple terms there are three broad consequences if an individual or business does not pay their share: either the contribution of others is increased, services for others are not delivered or investment in our future is curtailed. Tax is not something forced upon the people by some body over which they have no control. In our democratic society we elect government and in doing so we give them a mandate which includes that of setting taxation policy. You will all be familiar with the principle, first enshrined in the Magna Carta and later employed as a rallying call of the American revolution, of 'no taxation without representation'. It is also worth considering the corollary – that democratic representation is dependent on taxation.

Over the years, even though it has not been labelled as such, the concept of 'social capital' and attendant themes of community values, civic responsibility and the like have been very much on the minds (and in the hearts) of participants of Céifin conferences. In his bestseller *Bowling Alone*, Robert Putnam discusses the linkage between social capital and effective government and reports the results of a US study which concludes that 'social capital is the only factor that successfully predicts tax compliance'.[8] Richard Adams, writing in the *Guardian*, recently made the point that in the UK '… paying taxes has become the most patriotic duty undertaken by the majority of the population.'[9] In a transforming Ireland it is no less so.

Notes

1 Taken from his message as printed in the 2007 Céifin Conference Brochure.

2 'Survey of Small and Medium Sized Business Customers 2006: Results and Analysis', published by the Revenue Commissioners, January 2007 and available through www.revenue.ie.

3 Ibid.

4 G. Chryssides and J. Kaler, *Essentials of Business Ethics*, Maidenhead: McGraw–Hill, 1996, p. 10

5 André Comte-Sponville, *A Short Treatise on the Great Virtues*, UK: Vintage, 2003, p. 87

6 Doreen McBarnet, 'When Compliance is Not the Solution but the Problem: From Changes in Law to Changes in Attitude', Centre for Tax System Integrity, Research School of Social Sciences, Australian National University, 2001.

7 Frank Hussey, *The Irish Times* (Letters) 31 July 2004.

8 Robert D. Putnam, *Bowling Alone*, New York: Simon and Schuster, 2001, p. 347

9 Richard Adams, 'Cash in hand', *Guardian*, 12 August 2006.

How To Achieve Our Vision

A View from the Chair

Rachael English

Last year when the Leaving Cert results were released, amid all of the usual acres of newsprint about points and parties there was an interesting intervention from the Irish Business and Employers Confederation. On a day when, ordinarily, we can expect lots of platitudes about how well everybody has done, IBEC decided it was time for a different tack.

Far from school leavers never being brighter and never having so many opportunities, it expressed the view that too many eighteen-year-olds took little interest in their work and assumed that if they lost one job another would quickly come their way. Caroline Nash, who is assistant director of policy with IBEC, said that from an employer's point of view finding the right person for the job had never been more difficult. And she painted a picture of a teenage world where everybody is so busy texting and engaging in online chat that their grasp of English is worryingly limited. To be honest, I think many of us over the age of thirty probably had a sneaking sympathy with those views. In fact, it is not uncommon to hear the current generation of thirty-somethings bemoaning the attitude of those just a decade behind. The harshest criticism is often reserved for younger brothers and sisters who 'have it too easy' or 'can't just get a proper job and stick to it'. Indeed, I have one friend who has been known to express the view that 'a good recession' would sort a lot of young people out. And those views aren't just the stuff of pub chat. They have a practical manifestation. I have spoken to quite a few employers who have said that given the choice between a young Irish person and a young EU immigrant they would choose the immigrant because 'they're not afraid of work'. But I think it is time we were honest with ourselves. How much of this disdain is down to pure, old-fashioned envy? And how much of that envy is totally misplaced? One of the reasons I ask this is because around the same time that IBEC were expressing those views, I had to do a radio interview about the phenomenon of Internet 'networking' sites like BEBO and myspace. By that time I had done several such interviews and I have to admit I had never actually looked at any of the sites. So, for fear of sounding like the judge who asked, 'What is the Beatles?' I decided it was time to broaden my Internet education. It was quite a revelation. So many nights out, so many trips to Australia (such straight hair and such good teeth!). The other thing that struck me was that, even for those who have left school or college, there was hardly any mention of work. We have all heard the fears about such sites encouraging bullying and paedophilia. I reckon that for most of us they are far more likely to engender sadness for our lost youth.

All of this came to mind at this year's Céifin conference when taking part in a discussion with, and I really do not wish to patronise them, four incredibly articulate young people. Listening to the four – Kieran O'Malley, Sally Ann Flanagan, Daráine Mulvihill and Colm Hamrogue – it occurred to me that a lot of us tend to speak a lot of nonsense about those between the ages of fifteen and twenty-five. The four were, primarily, reporting on the discussions that had taken place at the first Céifin National Students' Conference. But, I think that anybody who was there will agree that their contribution was actually far broader than that. Their views and experiences were made all the more fascinating by their honesty. And, as somebody who spends a lot of time interviewing others, I reckon that such honesty is relatively rare. I think they also helped to explode a few myths. Some of these relate to quite simple things, such as third-level education. I know quite a number of people who are of the view, indeed I have been known to express it myself, that many young people stay at college for far too long and that this is confirmation of their laziness and inability to engage with the world of work. Not so, according to the panellists who spoke about the pressure to amass as many qualifications as possible. They said that no matter how well you did, there was always the feeling that you should achieve just that little bit more.

I was also taken by the panellists' ability to laugh at themselves. They know it is ridiculous that students should be complaining about the lack of car parking spaces. But, no matter how young you are, the pressure to have more, as well as to achieve more, is considerably more intense than it was ten or twenty years ago. Indeed, I reckon this ties in to something spoken about earlier in the day by David Quinn. He reflected on that fact that the word 'loser' has become the ultimate term of abuse. For me, though, the most important, the most revealing, part of the discussion was when we moved on to talk about why, when they are supposed to 'have it all', so many younger people suffer from depression. And why so many choose to take their own lives. Suicide remains the biggest killer of people under the age of thirty-five in Ireland. It is, of course, a hugely complicated issue. But for all of the TV and radio discussions, for all of the newspaper articles, you get the sense that mostly we only scratch the surface. Traditionally that discussion has focused overwhelmingly on young men, and given that so many more men than women take their own lives this has been entirely appropriate. However, anecdotal evidence would suggest that it is also increasingly a female issue. And this is borne out by the facts. The Irish Association of Suicidology recently reported that the number of women taking their own lives in the 15–24 age group has doubled over the past decade. The numbers, they say, are still small but the trend shouldn't be ignored. Sally Ann's description of her own experience of depression was not just moving, it was also enlightening and encouraging. I was going to say that it was brave, which it was, but you shouldn't have to be brave to talk about such things, and maybe that is a big part of the problem. For all of the talk about how Ireland has changed, we can still find it hard to be honest about issues such as depression and mental illness. We have probably moved on somewhat from the days when the favourite euphemism for all such issues was 'nerves', but it is clear that we still have some way to go.

It seems to me that we have particular difficulty coming to terms with the fact that this generation has any obstacles in their way, or has any issues to worry about. For sure, we have plenty of reasons to be envious – they do have more money, they do have more opportunity. However, if in many ways they are the most fortunate generation Ireland has seen, they are probably also the most patronised. Certainly that was something the four panellists felt quite keenly. All spoke about the propensity of people to rely on patronising platitudes when faced with the problems of the younger generation. And again, some of this was very funny. As Colm put it, not all problems are solved by a glass of water, a banana and a good night's sleep.

A Student Perspective

Rachael English The first Céifin National Students' Conference took place last month [October 2006] and was entitled 'Engaging with a Transforming Ireland – A Young Person's Perspective'. As the title indicates, it is the perspective of young people we are interested in. We have four young people present who are going to debate a number of issues. To a certain extent, last month's conference will provide a backdrop to today's debate, but will not be based exclusively on that conference.

To introduce the four people we have here today: Kieran O'Malley is the USI [Union of Students in Ireland] Western Area Officer; Sally Ann Flanagan is the Fine Gael Mayor of Tuam and the country's youngest mayor; Daráine Mulvihill is the young person's representative on the Council of State (interestingly, Mary Davis, who will be speaking after this particular session, is also on the Council of State); Colm Hamrogue is President of the Union of Students in Ireland, which I imagine is a tough task.

We will begin by discussing the proceedings at last month's conference and the sort of issues that were debated by people there. Kieran, I think you are going to bring us through some of the big issues that emerged over those few days.

Kieran The conference was held in GMIT in Galway and I was asked to get involved. I attended this [Céifin] conference last year. Then I was asked if I would get involved in organising it. So I was more than happy to and once Liam [Bluett, CEO Céifin] showed me the list of speakers I was absolutely delighted.

The first speaker was Tom Collins, Professor of Education in Maynooth. Tom spoke about the role of education and re-connecting young people with Irish society. One issue discussed was the prevalence of television in our lives. For example, most bars have televisions (as we can see with the bar down there), and so, as the students believed, there is more time for drinking and less time for talking. In many homes you'll often find two or three television sets. Years ago, as highlighted by one student, on a Sunday night the whole family would sit around and watch *Glenroe*. Now, three different people can be watching three different programmes in three different rooms of the house. Something else that came out of Tom Collins' speech was that fewer young people are getting involved in physical activities and are instead sitting at home playing PlayStation and watching television on their own. This is worrying, as if the innocence of childhood has disappeared.

The next speaker was John Lonergan and he created a very lively debate in all the breakout sessions. He told a lovely story about the water fountain in the Mountjoy womens' prison and how some people were giving out about it. He asked one of the prisoners what she thought of it or what it represented to her. She replied that the fountain was so important because it represents freedom and outside life and the better life she could hope for when she left. Paul Reynolds touched on some of these issues yesterday, like the lack of amenities and poor planning in large estates like Moyross in Limerick and Doughiska in Galway. There is a profound need for facilities there for young people.

Following this, Ciana Campbell chaired the session and we had Brendan Smith – 'Speedy' as he is affectionately known – the Community Education Officer for DERI [Digital Enterprise Research Unit based in NUIG] and also a former Student Union President in NUIG. He talked about what it was like back in the good old days of student activism. He is the man that brought the student bar to NUIG, while also introducing sex to Galway, as he said himself: he was selling condoms in the college. So, I suppose, a lot of students will be eternally grateful to Speedy! He was a brilliant speaker, so passionate that I think half the audience wanted to barricade themselves in the room afterwards and protest about something just for the sake of protesting. We had Colm Hamrogue, who is also on this panel, talking the next day, about what it was like back in the early eighties: Ivan McPhilips and other activists there, how things have moved on and how things have changed. I am sure we will discuss this later on. One particularly interesting thing Brendan spoke of was that a lot of the people that were involved in activism in the eighties are still involved. It just shows how important it is to get involved in things in college, leading hopefully to a life-long activism.

After that, we had a panel discussion. The members of the panel were Paul Kelly from Console, an organisation based in Dublin and Galway that provides support for families bereaved by suicide, and Seamus McGuinness, an artist and Ad Astra scholar in Suicide Studies in UCD. He showed us a very moving six-minute DVD. There was text rolling across the screen, outlining the number of people who had committed suicide in Ireland last year and he had pieces of a cut-up shirt representing all of these people suspended mid-air. It is hard for me to describe and I wouldn't do it justice but it opened a very interesting debate on the topic of suicide.

Resulting from the breakout session, one of the things that became clear was the need for students and for people in general to be made aware of how to help people who might be depressed or who might go on to commit suicide. There needs to be support services there for people to be able to help students. It is a very emotive issue and a serious issue, especially in the West of Ireland and among young men. After that, we had a student presentation from two welfare officers, one from the University in Galway and one from the IT in Athlone. They touched on various student issues. Some of the issues would have been covered on the panel discussion, like alcohol and young people and alcohol, and I'm sure we are going to go into detail on that in a while.

On Friday morning, all students were back again, all bright-eyed and bushy-tailed, and we had Brian Walsh hosting the session, former President of GMIT, now a city councillor in Galway. The first speaker was very interesting: Ben Preston, Student Union President in Queen's University, Belfast. He was talking about the decreasing numbers of students from the Republic going to college in the North and the issue of fees. It costs £3,000 a year to go to college in the North. Ben's contribution was great for students from the South who wouldn't necessarily be aware of the political issues north of the border. The next speaker was Colm Markey, the President of Macra na Feirme. Colm gave a fantastic presentation. He outlined the urban/rural divide as he saw it, and he said that we need to modernise Ireland and bring services to rural areas to prevent urban sprawl. He believes that there is a stigma attached to being a farmer and that people are passing over the opportunity, despite the fear that they are discontinuing a family tradition or are letting down the older generations. And he said because of the difficulties associated with farming today many often have to take on second jobs and this pressure is leading to more depression. This point led into and fuelled the debate on suicide and depression among young men, especially in rural areas. The next speaker was Colm [Hamrogue] so I am not going to steal his comments, but it was great to see the students getting so passionate and so active in that debate.

We were lucky after that to have the South African Ambassador HE Devikarani Priscilla Sewpal Jana talking about multiculturism. She believes we have created an uncomfortable society in Ireland. She believes that we need to learn from the South African example, and she outlined the need for education to change. She also put it that in the Irish or European curriculum we only learn about our own history and American history and very often we don't know about other cultures. We barely brush over them and this could lead to a certain ignorance among some people and that it would be much better for young people to be able to learn about other cultures. It would increase tolerance, she believes. One of the very interesting things that came out of the student breakout sessions was that apparently there is a fear when it comes to discussing multiculturalism. People are afraid of being viewed as racist if they try to attack the issues and to debate them in an intelligent way. The main thrust was that education is key; the young need to be educated and are not naturally or inherently racist. The conference finished with 'Telling My Story', something similar to this. We had Sally Ann here, the Mayor of Tuam. She was talking about activism and participation in politics. We had John Hyland, who is in the Students' Union in NUIG. He was also talking about student participation. We had David Burke. Some of you may have heard of David. He is from Salthill and was on the Salthill/Knocknacarra football team that won the All-Ireland Football Club Final last year. David is an accountant and he noticed that the stamp duty, which everybody has to pay at the end of the year on credit cards, culminated in a large amount of money going into the government coffers. He tried to set up a credit card for Salthill GAA Club to raise funds for charity while he was there and, as he was looking into this, he realised the money should be better channelled. This was set up as a kind of a slap on the wrist for banks really, but there is such a large amount of money that could do so much more if it was going to charity. So he has brought this to the government; he is bringing it in front of Oireachtas committees. He has Eddie Hobbs behind him so it is looking good. David has actually given up his job and he is concentrating on this full time. He hopes that it will be in the Budget for next year. Some people might say it is idealistic but we in the Students' Union of Ireland believe it is very worthwhile and a very achievable goal and we are doing our best to support him. I would encourage everyone to get behind him and you will hear more about this in the media. He is a very interesting guy, a lovely guy, and he plays football with Alan Kerins, the well-known footballer.

Rachael It must be a very interesting experience being on the Salthill/Knocknacarra football team. Is there anybody there who doesn't raise funds for charity or isn't involved in good work, because Alan Kerins spoke here last year about his Zambia fund.

Kieran I don't know how they have time for training and winning All Irelands and raising money for charity. He [David] is such a confident guy, he doesn't complain about things, he just gets out and does it. That's a brilliant attitude to have and I think the students really took to him and took to his confidence and his determination and I really hope that that guy succeeds. There were other speakers there on the day and the feedback was very good. The under-25s are such a significant proportion of the population, about 40 per cent, so it is vital to get their voice and, hopefully, the student conference will go from strength to strength.

Rachael Thanks very much for that Kieran, we'll take up on all of those themes with you, with Sally Ann and with Daráine in just a few moments. First of all, you mentioned Colm's contribution to that conference and you said it prompted quite a debate. What was it, Colm, that you actually spoke about that prompted this?

Colm Well, first of all, I took a historic view of education. If we look back to the 1960s, 7 per cent of school leavers went on to higher education, while today over 60 per cent of school leavers go to higher education. College is seen now as more of an experience rather than just an education. I also asked questions in the room as to why people went to college. I was at a meeting of the Higher Education Authority and I was talking to this woman for about six minutes and she told me her name twice, she told me every single academic achievement and scholarship and where her son had been and what he had done and what he had played about fifteen times in three minutes. So one of the reasons why students go to college is sometimes because parents drive them to go, and things are changing. Students go to college for the whole experience. Some of them go just to get an education, some of them go to get a better career, some of them for the experience, some of them go because they like clubs and societies and different sports and they pick and chose their institution, sometimes not on an academic basis but on the basis of what extra-curricular activities the college has to provide.

A few interesting debates went on about how active students were back in the 1960s as opposed to how active students are now and I think one of the things that became very evident to me is that we have changed a lot and representation of students has changed a lot. To take for example, I represent students on the Higher Education Authority of Ireland and we meet with the Minister for Education. When I was President in Sligo IT, I sat on the governing body and students are represented all throughout the different levels, from being a student and a class rep on course boards to the very highest echelons of the government. I feel there has been a change in the kind of consultation or collaboration basis with students on that. Maybe people aren't out protesting as much now because we are actually sitting at the tables talking.

Another issue that were raised was students and alcohol. I stopped in Mullingar last night and was talking to my cousin's wife and she asked if drink would be an issue at the conference. It seems to be a question everywhere I go. I feel that the term 'binge drinking' is a sexy media term for students drinking. I think one of the things we all have to be vigilant of is drink in our culture and not just among students. And I feel sometimes that students are a very easy group to target regarding drink. But it is a problem in nearly everyone's family in Ireland and I know, and am not afraid to say it, that there are people, not in my immediate family, but in my outside circle of family that have problems with drink. I believe it is something in Ireland's culture and I think it is something we need to look at.

Just following on from what Kieran has said, the presentation I gave in Galway was about my own experience in Galway or my own experience of going to college, as well as being involved in things from a young age. As well as sports I have been an active crew member in Bundoran Lifeboat for the last nine years. But when I was going to school, there were no PlayStations. You had one television in your house, you went out and you played sport with your friends and that's changing somewhat in Ireland. In fairness, there is no point in blaming anyone. A friend of my brother's has a ten-year-old son, and he would not go out and play football until he got a pair of boots that cost €130. Now who's at fault there, the parents or the son? Are the kids asking for too much or are the parents giving too much, and where do you draw the line? I think there needs to be a bit of a 50:50 split among things. We need to look at getting active and becoming involved in the community, returning to the notion of the 'Land of a Thousand Welcomes', where it's not all about the rat race and not just about making money. We need to instil this notion in kids when they are young. I know that if I had told my parents that I wouldn't play without a pair of €130 boots, I'd have been made to play in my socks!

The USI was very actively involved in the Taskforce on Active Citizenship and I was at one of the meetings. It wasn't directly with the Taskforce but it was an agency that was involved with the Taskforce, and I was discussing issues that were affecting young people and why young people are working so hard and working so many hours. One of the reasons was to be able to afford property. One person, who was the Chief Executive Officer of a Youth organisation, turned around and told me that this wasn't an issue for young people. But I know it's an issue because it's an issue for me. And I know that I don't have enough money to put down a deposit on a house. If we look at this over the years, so much has changed in comparison to when we were young. Maybe there's a move away in Ireland from the community, from knowing your neighbour or giving to your neighbour, to personal attainment and personal goals, getting the most you can to make the best you can. We were having a conversation over lunch about why people don't spend much time with others, like neighbours, and I know that when I moved up to Dublin I even lost time for myself because, for example, I spent so much time in traffic. You work the maximum amount of hours you can to get the most amount of money you can because it is so expensive to live there. It turns into a vicious circle. I think we need to look today at how to curb this vicious circle.

Rachael We are going to go to Daráine and Sally Ann in just a moment but I want to pick up on something you said, Colm, about drink and about whether that was something really unique to young people or whether it had always been the same? I want to put to you a point that a senior administrator in a Dublin University made to me a couple of years ago, and I have a feeling you mightn't like this. He said that he blamed a lot of the student drinking culture on the fact that students no longer have to pay fees. He argued that students have more money and that they spend that money on alcohol and, as someone who runs a college, he was praying for the day when fees would be brought back. What would you say to that?

Colm Well, there's a few different points that I can take because I think I know the person you're talking about. I think I had this debate on *The Last Word* on Today FM with him already this year. The re-introduction of fees brings us to the point of actually accessing education and people not getting into education and if you were to reintroduce fees, this would be the case for many. If you brought in fees of €10,000, students are going to find the money to get a pint somewhere on a Wednesday night. If you brought in fees of €20,000, students are going to find the price of a pint. You ask someone paying off a mortgage and maybe a fancy car if they'd like a drink, and they too will find the money somewhere.

Rachael I think his point was maybe not that students wouldn't find money for a pint because, of course, they would, but maybe they wouldn't find money for ten pints.

Colm Well, that might be the point he's putting, but there's a whole thing now in Ireland about how students are wealthier and all of that. Ireland is a richer economy now than it was ten years ago. It's far richer, and we look at it and see that students spend €100 on a night out. Maybe €100, I'm not sure what its equivalent was fifteen years ago. It might be £20/£30 that students could have been spending back then. Taking that into consideration, that's maybe a 60 or 70 per cent increase but in actual value terms it's not that much. Now I realise the point you are putting forward but I really don't think that the re-introduction of fees would curb any drinking problems.

Rachael Can I ask you then, Daráine, about something mentioned by Colm, and this is probably unfair, but there is this perception, maybe amongst people who either went to college or perhaps, more importantly, didn't go to college twenty or thirty year ago, that you all have it handy nowadays?

Daráine It's ridiculous. The newspapers, especially the tabloids, are full of sensational stories about young people, with accompanying photographs posed by models. And it's just not representative of the life of a student at all. We still have the hours, long hours, in lectures up to 6/7 o'clock at night and then projects and then exams, and the stress! Students don't have the time to be going out; they might go out once a week. On the issue of money, I don't think students have more money. I think the bars and pubs are charging so much for drink now that a lot of students are drinking at home.

Rachael You have just started work after a number of years at college. What has changed in your life?

Daráine I spent three years doing a degree in DCU and last year I did a post-graduate course in NUIG. The degree and the post-graduate course were completely different because the course I did last year is actually pretty similar to the job I am doing now. It was a full-time job practically, just without the money. In terms of the degree, you did have more freedom. You could do things like we were talking about, such as clubs and societies. It could be active. I was very active in my college in a number of the clubs and societies. You do need that time to be involved in those kinds of things because I think that's what changes you as a person. I am just finished college, but already when I look back, it's the events that I remember, it's the times with my friends, it's the clubs and societies, the different things we did. You don't remember the academics; college is just a way of getting your degree to get the job. I don't think a lot of what you learn is for life. I think it's the experiences of college that's important.

Rachael Would you have thought then that some of your fellow students were so het up in the academic side of things that they might end up regretting that they didn't do other things.

Daráine Already I know some people in my class that say they regret it because they were so focused. There is such a focus, like there was on the Leaving Cert, that leads into college. That has become such a huge issue for young people nowadays. You hear of students having breakdowns at seventeen because there is so much pressure. I don't know is it the media or the parents or who it is applying this pressure but it leads into college then because people have to achieve the grades. There are just so many more people in college now competing because only a certain amount are going to get the top marks and some people really feel under pressure to get those marks.

Rachael So how do you feel then when you hear people saying that the points are on the way down, that life is going to get easier from now on?

Daráine It's not, I think it's just getting worse and worse. Like when we spoke about primary school kids being given so much, getting everything they want. There is going to be so much stress on them when they reach our age, when they reach their late teens, early twenties.

Rachael I am going to come back to Colm in a moment but Sally Ann, we've been talking with Daráine about getting involved in things. Now, you're in a relatively unusual position in that you're quite a young person involved in party politics. You are the Mayor of Tuam. Would you know many people your age who think, 'God, Sally Ann, she must be mad'?

Sally Ann Yes, a lot! I have to say when I was asked to go for the Town Council I thought it was quite mad! I thought they must be joking. And then when I thought about it I just weighed up the pros and cons and went for it. At first, as you said, people thought I was mad, but after I was elected, a lot of people came up to me and said it was great. They also came for information, for example, on how to make a presentation to a member of the Town Council. But when I was in school I never thought politics was something I'd get into. And I certainly didn't think I'd get into it at such a young age. And now I wonder why I thought this. It was just because I wasn't asked and it's because young people aren't asked or approached to go for it. My mother's friend asked me to go forward and I am eternally grateful to her now.

Rachael Amongst many people you knew growing up, would party politics have had a bad image? I know from talking to many young people in recent years that they have no interest per se in party politics but are interested in the environment and in Third World debt and areas like that. Do people view party politics as squalid almost?

Sally Ann Some do have a bad opinion of party politics. Of course you look at the news and every evening they are discussing some tribunal so it's easy to get pessimistic. But it is very encouraging to see people with an interest in politics. For example, when I did history so many of the girls in my class were really interested in Irish politics and just wanted to learn more and more. We were actually the first year to do CSPE [Civil, Social and Political Education] and the amount of people who were interested in it was just unbelievable. I was even talking to a teacher in Tuam and she is teaching CSPE and she asked me to come into the class because the class wanted to get involved in junior projects in the town and learn more about politics. So I don't think it's the case that a lot of young people hate politics. It's that they're not well enough informed and are not being educated in the right way.

Rachael Colm, I think you were keen to come in on a couple of the points made by Daráine, perhaps about getting involved in activities and about the lives of young people nowadays?

Colm There's two points I would like to add. The first, regarding getting involved, is what's known as Accreditation for Participation. I know that a lot of students were involved in this from my days in the Students' Union in DCU. Basically, if you participate in your clubs or societies or student union or volunteering at college, it actually adds to your academic accreditation so you achieve something additional on your degree. I think it's a carrot offering, you know, in that here's something that will recognise your contribution to college. Last year, DCU won the Sigerson [Cup: GAA football competition] and Sligo, my college, won it the year before that, and there is a huge amount of prestige attached to the college for winning these types of things. It's the students that are out training on the pitch at 7 a.m. and 8 p.m., in between their studies, that are achieving that success for the college, and this success the college markets for itself. So I think that the college recognising the students' participation and value is a great step forward.

Another point I want to carry on from Sally Ann, and it was something that I brought up in my presentation. When I was the President of Sligo IT, I was very heavily involved in the strategic plan for the college. Over four months I sat down with 250 students and I interviewed them about why they weren't involved. I asked them, basically, what three short-term issues they wanted to see resolved and what three long-term key issues they would like included in the strategic plan. I got an awful lot of reluctance from people to thinking long-term about what they wanted. The main consensus, and I think it was about 82 per cent, as to why students wouldn't think that far down the road or get involved was that it doesn't sort out the day-to-day problems. This comes back to the problem of grants for students. Those who are on grants are so because of their income limit and the income limit of their parents. Not to go on a political spiel here, but the welfare of the student must be protected. Those getting the grant are getting it for a reason and we mustn't forget that. The grant problem has been around since the 1960s and it hasn't been fixed. But what they reiterated again and again in Sligo when I asked them about local issues and national issues and long term and short term was that they [the politicians] don't want to fix the day-to-day problems that affect our lives. I think it is somewhat expected in Ireland for things to be late, or over budget and all of that. What we are trying to explain to students, just in my own capacity as USI President, coming up to a general election is that politics is not just 166 people sitting on red chairs in Dáil Éireann. For students, and for everyone else, it is how safe we are on the streets. That's politics. How good is our health care system, how good is our public transport? How good is our infrastructure? This is what we are relaying to students, making it relevant and tangible. As Sally Ann said, there is disbelief among some people about why they won't just sort out the issues rather than campaigning on them. That was just some of the information that was fed to me at the Sligo Planning process.

Rachael I asked Sally Ann actually about that point. This perception is certainly very prevalent among young people. It would seem to me that politicians spend more time knocking spots off each other than they do trying to solve problems.

Sally Ann Well, I suppose, when you look at Dáil Éireann and see Leaders questions, you can see that happening. I got into politics because I wanted to do something for my town. I wanted to give something back to my town. It wasn't because I looked at the Dáil on the telly one night and said ... (**Rachael** I'd like to slag off Fianna Fáil!)

Sally Ann It's not like that and I think to be perfectly honest, I'd hate to think that I would slag people off just to make myself look better. I think I am better than that. But it happens on both sides. Though I am with Fine Gael, even if I was with Fianna Fáil, it doesn't mean I would do the exact same thing as Enda Kenny or Bertie Ahern. I am a different person. I hope I am bringing a fresh image to politics and a lot of my own friends do find it is more approachable and easier to talk about. I just give a different perspective on it.

Rachael Kieran, what is your view?

Kieran Well, I'd like to bring it back to the issue of drink. We have to look at the broader picture. Why are students drinking? Is it because of this lack of confidence, lack of self-esteem or are they lonely? But what we are looking at now is the pressure students are under, like with modularisation, semesterisation, I mean, it's non-stop. You have thirty-five hours a week. You have presentations and you have projects on top of this. There is such a workload in college that it is no wonder students get to a Thursday night, go out and get smashed. And that's terrible. I'd prefer to have a few pints in the pub. I love going out and having the craic but you want to have a conversation. Now the price of drink is gone up and maybe that is one of the factors as to why people are drinking at home and it's definitely happening now. There's cheap drink, alco pops, wine. People are drinking at home because they don't want to be paying the pub prices and just want to get into the nightclub. So they are going into the nightclubs and they are hammered drunk, the music is so loud, they are falling around the place. You can't really talk to people or strike up conversations, and this unnamed president of DCU (**Rachael** He wasn't actually the president of DCU, he was one of his right-hand men) is talking about if students have less money then they won't go out drinking. So what do we want, do we want socially retarded individuals that go into class, come out as machines? I went to college, I had brilliant craic. I was involved in soccer, Gaelic and different clubs and societies. I wouldn't have been a model student ever but I enjoyed myself and I think I came out a better, more rounded individual. I thought class parties were the best part of college because you could socialise with the class, making it easier in group presentations the next time to strike up conversation. So I think we need to bring in students or to develop students that are more rounded, holistic individuals.

For my sins, I am in charge of the Ladies' Football team in GMIT and have been for seven years now. When I started, we'd go and play the match and we'd have the craic for the day. Now I find players turning down anything but the game as they've course work or they've to be up early in the morning for lectures. There were twenty students from GMIT here yesterday, but very few back today because many can't miss two days of college. The women's football team have a fantastic sponsorship deal from PF Sports, and I've had to use this as bribery. It's gone to that stage where they want to play a sport and they want to be involved but they are under so much pressure and they're there to get an education.

But as a person I wouldn't have developed as much if I hadn't got involved in, say, soccer and I think it is so important to encourage participation. All of us have been involved in different things and I think this came out in the 'Telling My Story' discussion at the conference. We had people who were involved in charity, involved in students' union, involved in politics and there needs to be a spark there, there needs to be infrastructure. For me it was to become a chairperson of the soccer club in college and that helped my organisation skills and led into different things. There needs to be structures there, a way for students to channel their abilities and their interests and to be able to develop as a person who wants to move on to other aspects.

Rachael Can I go back to something actually, Kieran, that you said right at the start. You spoke about a student's life or life for a lot of students being that they work incredibly hard and they put in long hours. They have assessment projects and then feel as if they need to go out and get absolutely hammered. In some ways, that sounds more like working life than a student's life used to be. It's almost like you get older younger.

Kieran That's what I'm seeing now. Once you hit fifteen, it's all about the Leaving Cert, and you are concentrating on that. When I was younger, my parents were bringing me to football practice and other sports. Now, kids are being brought to grinds. You go into college and if you miss one lecture, you are in trouble. There is so much pressure now, especially with this modularisation. You are doing twelve subjects a year – you do six subjects before Christmas, you have your exam and you move on to do the next six subjects. So it's hard to miss time and, if you do, you are falling behind the rest of the course. Even presentation of projects is being done to such a high standard. For example, when my thesis was due in fourth year, some of the girls in my class had a meeting to discuss which weight of paper was going to be used and where they were going to get it bound. Everything was so professional and so well done that you'd swear we were working for a top company. It's crazy in a way. Obviously, it prepares you well for working life but at the same time it puts you under so much pressure, and people need to look around and be concerned about different things. It's a shame that people don't seem to have the time to do this anymore.

Rachael Daráine, can I ask you about being the young person's representative on the Council of State. What does it involve, because it is quite an unusual position to be in.

Daráine It's more an honorary role and it was an honour to be asked. Basically, the Council of State has been in existence since the constitution of Bunreacht na hÉireann. When President

McAleese took office, she wanted to have a young person on the Council. The President already appoints seven lay people to the Council; some are involved in the Dáil or Seanad. President McAleese asked me to be the representative for her second term in office. So it's been four years now since I started. It involves going to the meetings and speaking on a topic that maybe affects young people. It's to have a young person's perspective at these meetings, a different angle or point of view.

Rachael Can I ask you all about something, obviously a far darker subject, but a subject I know came up on several occasions at your own conference. It's very hard to talk about young people these days without talking about the problem of suicide and sometimes it's very hard to know what to say. I know the media often has trouble even reporting suicide because it is very hard to get it right. This was something, Colm, that came up at the conference. What sort of contributions did people make?

Colm The first point that I want to make is that, as a student, there is as much required and demanded of us as if we were young professionals in any given field. As Kieran said, with the presentation of reports, the standard that is required is of a similar quality to what would be expected of professional consultants. These are the standards we have to produce. There is so much pressure put on young people now from a young age to get ahead from the Leaving Cert. Then once the Leaving Cert is over, it's getting into college. And once you are in college, it's getting the best project and getting the best degree and then a post-graduate degree, because we hear so much talk about fourth-level education. And it's just building; it seems that nothing is good enough now. Where is it going to stop? I know when I was doing my degree there was an awful lot of pressure. What's important is the mental health of students. That is the key that we need to look out for. We are currently running a campaign called 'Mind Yourself'. It's to know what the telltale signs are. As we become a more open, more vocal Ireland, depression is not the closeted subject it was twenty years ago, when people used to pass it off with, 'Sure, he's suffering from the nerves, God love him'. We all know now that it's an open thing and it's OK to talk about it. It is something we all have a responsibility to look out for. People may appear happy, normal, chatting but they can still be depressed. I think one of the most crucial things is that we have to be careful of how much we actually ask. Also, as Kieran said, we need to be aware of the pressures of the whole education system and the modulation that seems to be filtering down from practices in Europe. This means basically that, in my case, my Level 8 degree (there is a range of degrees) will be recognised in Germany, and will be of the same value in Spain. So it allows for free open access of the European market. But with this comes a serious workload and serious pressure and demands on students to get projects, assignments and exams done and you have to meet the criteria to progress and all of that. Students need to be offered support in dealing with their own mental well being and welfare.

Rachael How do you go about providing that support?

Colm Well, just to take a look at campus support. There are counsellors on campus. There are the Samaritans. Local student unions have welfare officers with campaigns and they run that. Within the college there are counsellors, nurses and doctors. All provide that support. But sometimes, students don't realise that they are depressed or that they are under so much pressure or anxiety or stress. That is why it comes back to the issue of being an active citizen and looking out for your friends and looking out for those people who are beside you and making sure that Joe or Ann or whoever is doing alright. The information is out there and we all know it. We all have to do our own wee bit first, before we start looking outside the box, before we start criticising parents or students or anything. Maybe we all just need to take a look inside ourselves and ask could we give an extra 10 per cent, and with that extra 10 per cent just lift the bar that little bit more, and if we lift the bar a little bit more would society become better and would things just ease? Maybe it's a thing, and I feel very strongly about this, that we just need to look at ourselves first to see where we are rather than criticising everyone and everything around us. Maybe it's a thing where everyone needs to take a look at where they are at and just see if they can individually give that little bit more.

Rachael Daráine, Colm mentioned one of those great Irish euphemisms, 'he suffers from the nerves'. There is the perception, I think, and there must be some truth in this because fewer young women do commit suicide, that young women are better at talking about their problems if they are a bit down or if they are suffering from depression. Is that your experience with your friends? Would you believe that girls are better at talking about things, or is there more pressure now to be seen as super successful that even young women are scared to talk about these things.

Daráine No, I think young women are still pretty open about things. I think young men are becoming better as well. There is much more awareness. I know when I was in secondary school we had people come in to talk to us about suicide and depression because it is such a problem in Ireland. So we have been aware of it and the symptoms since we were quite young. I think most people are OK about talking about these things. I think for young men it is always going to be the same. There's going to be the whole macho image, they don't want to seem the sensitive type. But it is slowly changing. You see the two guys here are well able to talk. I think it is just a perception. The same as everything else, there are always stereotypes but I can see an improvement.

Sally Ann The issue of suicide is very important to me as I have known people who have committed suicide. A girl, a friend of mine, committed suicide during the summer. Even my own first cousin, years ago, committed suicide. A lot of people are very reluctant to talk about it and because of that people don't want to admit that they did suffer from depression. My sister died when I was nine. Then in secondary school I suffered very badly from depression. I used to wake up in the morning not wanting to get out of the bed. I used to go to bed and actually pray to God that I wouldn't even wake up. And the only reason, I think, that I never took it any further was because I saw how upset my mother and father were when my sister passed away. And I loved them so much I could never do that to them. But yet still I felt I was such a burden on everyone and that I was such a burden on my friends that I couldn't talk to them. I felt like I was dragging them down by talking to them. It was only when speaking with a career guidance counsellor in school that it became too much. She asked me what I wanted to do with my Leaving Cert. I just broke down. I went to counselling then after that and I have become much stronger since. But I do know a lot of people that suffer from depression and I think it's still a hidden subject, I really do. And it really upsets me because there are a lot of brilliant people out there who have taken their lives because they felt they were too much of a burden, that they didn't want to be troubling others with their problems when, in fact, it was the opposite. And it is people who are left behind that are left wondering. I know a guy at home studying medicine who was under a lot of pressure, but it was pressure he was putting himself under, as with my best friend: she is studying medicine and when it comes around to exam time I'm petrified. She is a fantastic person but it's just that I am aware of the pressure and I am aware of what it was like to be depressed. I don't really care about saying it now because I think so many people keep it a secret. I felt like I was going into court when I was going into the doctor to get anti-depressants. I felt, 'Oh my God, how do I say this?' It was so, so tough. And when I went in the doctor said it is so, so common. It is so common.

Rachael Was that a big relief for you at the time, even to have a name on it and for a doctor to say, 'Listen, this is quite common, you are not unusual'?

Sally Ann It definitely was a relief, so much so that I even told one of my friends. I didn't feel so bad about actually having to say it.

Then I found out that a lot of people I knew actually had suffered from depression as well. And I found that because I had said it a lot of people started to say things to me as well. It is quite scary, I have to say, and I do think drink has a lot to do with many suicides that happen. I was out one night and I got a text from a friend of mine and I literally had to run to their house and bang on their door until they let me in. And that is a really scary feeling but you would never think that that person ever suffered with depression.

Rachael You must have tons of self-confidence to be doing the job you are doing now.

Sally Ann A lot of people think that but I mean you know the song, 'Tracks of my Tears': the person you think could never be suffering from depression might just be that person. You just have to be very conscious of it. I am because I knew people who committed suicide and I suffered from depression myself. I think people need to be very open about it but it is so common and I know for a fact that it is very easy to get down about things nowadays. I have the pressure of being mayor, and it's great, but I hope that if anything came out of the year it would be that others are encouraged by my role and encouraged to strive themselves.

Rachael It would be a great thought! Kieran, what are your own views on this subject? You worked with so many students, you must have been in a situation from time to time when you know somebody is suffering and you don't know how to intervene?

Kieran Absolutely. I worked as a welfare officer in the Students' Union in GMIT in my first year as a sabbatical. It was definitely something that we were trained for. USI organise training for us as welfare officers. I mean, we are not doctor, counsellor, or priest. I find that I'm a fairly good listener so that is what I tried to do for students: to be there and to have an open door policy. I went around the college and tried to be as friendly as possible so that the students would be able to come in and feel able to talk. On a larger scale, there was always a Welfare Week in GMIT where people could pick up leaflets from one stand in the canteen. But if there are only leaflets for the Samaritans in this one stand, you're not really going to march over and take one. So I organised it on a much larger scale. I had fifty different companies like Bodywise, Kelloggs, Sniffer Dogs Drug Squad, all with leaflets, and maybe then in the middle of this was information on the Samaritans and a box of sweets beside it. People could go over on the pretence of taking sweets or looking up the different companies, and then maybe get information on the Samaritans. Students need to realise that the information is out there, but it needs to be accessible. It cannot be made obvious. There's a lovely lady outside, Margaret, who is working with Console, and Paul Kelly, who set up Console, was speaking at the student conference. His speech was very moving because he told us that the organisation came about following the suicide of his sister. They provide support services for families to help them deal with grief and take them through the grieving process in an effort to move on and bring the families back together. These organisations are invaluable for these families. They are registered charities. I've just taken up a directorship on the Galway Youth Federation, which is over all the youth charities in Galway. We do everything we can to support these charities. I've had a very fortunate life. I have never had to deal with any of these problems. But there are people who haven't been so fortunate. As a welfare officer I have dealt with some students and I don't know how they got through college. Personally it was great to have friends who were outside college, outside the situation, to be able to talk to. It's great to have people who know the circumstances you are going through as well.

It is just so important that we try and get involved in the support services that are there for people. We are talking about young men being afraid to talk, though I think it has improved. I actually think the mobile phone has been invaluable in this. I have friends who are working all over the place and they'd ring me up and talk utter rubbish. But it's good to chat to them and it's good to talk to people and keep in touch and you know they're happier than sitting in their hotel room all night, away from home, not talking to anyone. It is a problem and it is a serious problem. Young men still do not communicate enough. I don't really like to open up or talk about my feelings but I still have a very strong support network of friends that I can talk to if I have problems. I think that lads are beginning to develop that. I think going to college helped like that, meeting new people and experiencing new things. But I have been lucky. Through the Students' Union you see what goes on in other peoples' lives and you realise how lucky you are and how you need to use the services that are there to try and improve things.

Rachael Just a thought, Daráine: I suppose the challenges you had yourself growing up were quite different in many ways because they were physical challenges as a result of the illness you had. But maybe in some way there is a kind of similarity because I suppose you had to battle a wee bit as well.

Daráine Yes, I was just thinking about that. I didn't have a disability until I was sixteen, until I got meningitis. So I could see from both sides the perspectives and I think similar to the issue of depression and suicide, the issue of disability is coming more to the forefront. Maybe twenty years ago there weren't many people with disability in college or in the workforce but now there are. I think the services are in place now in college to help people with disabilities. But I think that there's still stigma attached to it.

Rachael Is there some condescension as well, with people saying, 'isn't she great!'?

Daráine Yeah, maybe with a lot of young people who mightn't have come across disability. People are more open now about it though, and maybe come across it more in college. It's great that it's more open because it leads to people discussing issues and those with disabilities becoming more integrated, and others realising that there's no difference. I'm aware of this especially because once

175

I hadn't a disability and now I do and I am exactly the same person. The whole idea of focusing on the disability is wrong. I think you need to focus on the person and what they have to say. Often you'll read an article in the paper about someone with a particular disability and there'll be a huge photograph focusing on this. Whereas I think it is better to focus on the person.

Rachael You probably know Eoin McGowan who works in RTÉ and presents a radio programme for people with disabilities. He had a great line on it. He had an accident in his early twenties, and subsequently had to use a wheelchair and he said, if you know somebody with a disability it's probably the least interesting thing about them.

Daráine I think people forget to focus on the 'ability': you have to think of what they are able to do. Disability can be anything. In college disability is classed as anything from dyslexia to being fully paralysed. There are different strains of it and it's just that there's a stigma. It is something that a lot of young people nowadays are more educated about and aware of. I find they'll accept you much more readily than many older people.

Rachael It's an interesting point. I'd like to ask one more question: What is the one thing you would change about older people's perception of young people. What is the biggest misconception out there as far as you are concerned?

Colm I'm looking out at a lot of older people so I'll be careful! One of the things I want to highlight is that we do get a raw deal in the media. I know that the pressures we face are different from what people of an older generation faced. I know from my own parents, like my father laughing at me when I tell him I have been looking at my computer all day. I come home even from my job as President of the Union of Students and my father, who has a haulage contractor business, says that if I had to drive to Cork and back again I'd know a real day's work! He doesn't understand what it is like to sit in an office for ten hours. Sometimes it is just understanding young people and the pressures that we face. Sometimes I find that the older generation's attitude is, 'Arrah, sure you'll be grand, there'll be not a loss on you'. My mother's resolve to everything is if you get to bed and get a good night's sleep, you'll be grand. If everything was that simple in life!

Just before I wrap up: when I was eighteen and halfway through my Leaving Cert, I was involved in a hit and run car accident. I broke my back and was in hospital for five months after it. When I came out of hospital after four and a half months, I was very institutionalised and I was in a body brace. You become very reliant on the doctors in that little bubble. When I came out and when I was totally out of the hospital care and everything, I found it very hard to cope and I was having panic attacks. And my mother would be saying, you're fine, take a glass of water, go to bed, wake up in the morning and you'll forget about it, eat a banana, you're not eating enough fruit! If she had been saying, 'you don't look great this morning', that would really tip the boat. I went for counselling after some bad panic attacks on the suggestion of my doctor, and when a doctor suggests something like this you take their word for it. When I walked into the counsellor's office I said, 'I think I'm going crazy' but the counsellor reassured me and said it was completely normal after such trauma. Even after this initial consultation I was so relieved. My point is that it is very difficult for young men to express themselves and admit when something is wrong. It seems that men and women are just completely different and men just find it more difficult to talk. But today in Ireland there are a lot more support services, like the Samaritans, and these are much more accessible than in the past. With the Samaritans an address like joe@samaritans.ie will get you in contact immediately, and it's easy to find people on the Internet.

Still, it's trying to get the older generation to appreciate the difficulties faced by younger people today. Because many of the older generation don't have the mortgages on their houses, or have to get on the career ladder, or decide if a BA will suffice or will an

MA have to be undertaken, they don't see the many pressures and decisions being faced by young people today. The challenges that we face are much different and it would be great if we could see a greater acceptance of these challenges. For example, if I were to go home and say to my mother that I'd had a hard day staring at the computer for ten hours, and she replied that that must have been hard, maybe I'd be quicker in filling up the coal bucket! If I could just get across one thing: there needs to be a greater understanding and I think it would be something that the younger generation would appreciate.

Rachael Daráine, any thoughts?

Daráine I am mainly interested in the media because I am working in it at the moment. I think the media has a huge role to play in how young people are perceived. I think people need to realise, and I'm sure most people know, that selling a newspaper is always about having the sensational headline. You are always going to turn a story to the agenda that you want and young people always come out the worst in those kind of media articles. So I just think that people need to look to those young people doing good: in the colleges, clubs and societies, all run by young people with great enthusiasm and spirit and with so much energy. The negative images aren't the reality and if young people were encouraged more, who knows what they would do. Just look at the Mayor of Tuam here beside us: she is only a student, and people may laugh at the concept, but she is as good and better than many of the other mayors throughout the country.

Rachael Would the Mayor of Tuam like to add to that?

Sally Ann I suppose, to disregard the youth element, we are all people trying to get along in the world. With my parents, they are very understanding and they actually feel sorry for young people. While some people say young people are this, that and the other, you have to think as well that not all older people are the same. There are a lot of people that are very understanding and know the pressures that young people are under. According to films and stories, the sixties were a pretty wild time! You can't be hypocritical either. You have to realise that everyone was young and everyone went out and had a laugh. If people could just leave aside the idea that this is a young person's world. I am a young person: at what point do I stop being young? At what point do I go into the 'old' bracket? We are all people, we are all trying to get on.

Kieran I suppose I'll be really boring and have something to say to the politicians. I am from a tiny village, Bonniconlon. It's seven miles from Ballina and I love that village. Unless I go home and play in goal, there is nothing really I can contribute. I'd love to be able to go home and work in Bonniconlon and promote and improve the local area. We need the government to cash in on these commitments. There are reports on everything. Everything is a great idea – the West is brilliant, the wealth, the rail corridor, broadband, everything. It's just to follow through with some of these things. There are so many gifted and talented young people. You have three of them here. I have met so many people in college who are so talented and so brilliant and do feel like wanting to contribute to their own community but are not able to. They have to go to Dublin. It's easy for me to get involved in things in Galway and that's a great grounding for me. But I'd love to be able to go home and do some of the things that I have learned and try to promote the community at home and try to get involved. I have been involved in GMIT and in USI and I want to be involved at home to make things better for other people. But there is nothing there for me to do. There's probably no job for me anyway. I don't know if I'll get a job when I'm finished. It's the need for infrastructure, support. It's up to the government. You know, we are going to hear all these great things coming up to the election. Do it, give us a chance in the West of Ireland and in rural areas to go back and give something to our communities.

Rachael Thank you all very much.

Together, We're Better

Mary Davis

I had a speech ready but as I went through the day and listened to everybody I realised that an awful lot of what I have prepared was already being expressed by speaker after speaker. I decided to just take a few notes about the various things that came up and hopefully now I'll be briefer in terms of what I am going to say, maybe giving time at the end for others because there is a lot of richness in this room, people who have done a huge amount of work in many fields. I would be really interested as chairman of the Taskforce on Active Citizenship to get an opportunity to hear your opinions on various things. I am particularly interested in how we are going to move forward, how we are going to change things and make things happen.

I want to congratulate Fr Harry Bohan on producing this fantastic conference year after year. Every year I think it gets better, enriching all of us. It is just so absorbing and so stimulating and so much food for thought. I had heard about Harry for a long time but I really only got to know him when he was serving on the Taskforce on Active Citizenship. The richness he brings to that committee is just incredible and when he's absent I really miss his input. I was taken by Alice when she talked about cascading the processes of excellence, and she mentioned that we all mightn't know what that means. But Harry speaks to everyone, young or old, in the same, straight-forward way. I really appreciate the flavour you bring to the Taskforce in doing that, Harry, and thank you for it.

On this point, I would also think that young people bring this simplicity also. They don't talk in convoluted language and that is great. I was in Tullamore at one of the public consultations on active citizenship and a young person was asked what it meant to be an active citizen and she said it was 'just doing good stuff without feeling that you are being forced to do it'. And I thought, yes, that's a really nice way of explaining active citizenship. It is about doing 'good stuff' and it is about doing it because you want to, like we see here today with our four young people. It is about contributing and not having somebody pushing you into doing it. You should do it because you want to do it.

I was struck by John Quinn's urgency. The whole urgency culture that he mentioned. The three mobile phones and the fact that we have no time to stop and stare. The example then on the other hand of the young fellow firing stones and reminding us that maybe sometimes it is a good idea to have nothing to do at all. It reminded me of the two Kerry men who were in Muckross Park working, one digging a hole, the other filling it in. Two Americans were wandering by and they thought, jeepers, that's intriguing, I wonder what they're doing, one digging a hole and the other filling it in. So, curiosity got the better of them and they decided to go over and ask. So, the two men lean on their shovels and said, 'Well, you know usually there's three of us, the third guy plants a tree, but he's off sick today'. So, there you go, there are some people who do nothing. The important thing, and I'll come back to it later on, is how do we fill our days? We are all busy busy, but the important thing is how do we fill our days? I am going to park that question just for the moment.

We have heard it all over the two days here at Céifin. The past was mapped out very well by David Quinn and then by John Quinn. He gave some wonderful descriptions of the Ireland of fifty years ago, and growing up in Mayo, like two of my colleagues, I knew all about the *meitheal* and what that did and how it was created and the co-ops as well as the wonderful co-operative effort. But we also heard the not-so-good side as well.

We've heard about today, twenty-first century Ireland, time-deficit Ireland, the violence, the road deaths, the people lying in hospital corridors, the shootings, the drugs, the children spending time separated from their parents and parents feeling guilty and lavishing perhaps more material goods because of this guilt.

We heard also from Alice especially about bureaucracy being alive and well. She talked about the endless forms, the policies and procedures, the governance, answering machines, the virtual world. I was listening to the radio yesterday while driving and I heard that you can now go on a virtual holiday from your office. There are virtual rooms now that children can go into and communicate. You don't have to gather in your own bedroom to talk anymore, you can just go to the computer, you can create your own room, the most beautiful room that you want to in the world and you can chat to your friends so that you don't have to take them into your own room. So, of course, with all of that, modern life is challenging.

Sometimes there is a tendency to look back over twenty, thirty, fifty years in a very nostalgic way and look at present-day Ireland with a sort of cynicism. There is also a tendency to compare sometimes. And just as we should never compare our children, each one distinct, so too, I believe, we should never compare the past with the present. Rather, we should use the richness of the past to influence the present. There were a lot of bad news stories from past Ireland; now we seem to hear of a new shooting every day, but back then it was shootings in Northern Ireland, it was the haemorrhaging of young people because of the lack of employment. There was no talk of returning to live in the West of Ireland because there were no opportunities there. It was an unstable time politically. Our young people were not so cherished. There may have been good times in a lot of ways, but there were also bad times. Our collective responsibility is how to get over those challenges and I think that's our real challenge. So how do we get over those? Now, I am also going to park that but I'll come back to it.

The second thing I would say, and Daráine mentioned it in reference to the media, is to recognise, to seek out, to acknowledge, to print, to talk about, to shout about the great things that are being done. We do hear about a lot of the negative things that are happening and it's a lot of what we hear on the radio or read in the papers. I would challenge the media, and I am not critical of it as it does report the good news. I saw first-hand, as I'm sure all of you did, the outpouring of love, of joy, during those World Games in 2003 when so many people, 30,000 people, 177 communities, came together, gave their time and their talents, gave their energy, their resources, would have stood on their heads, would have done anything to make those games successful. They did it simply because somebody went out and asked them, 'Will you help us, this is what's happening in Ireland'. The response was yes, yes, yes and how much more can I do for you.

We listened to Alice Leahy this morning – the same thing, huge amount of work being done in that area. I was in Monaghan recently launching a volunteer centre and I went to the Aontas centre, the most magnificent centre on the outskirts of Castleblaney, and it was a hive of activity. I discovered it was spearheaded by a nun called Sr Celine McArdle. She has done great work in that centre but also in the town of Castleblaney where there are issues of alcoholism and domestic violence and other problems. The energy she has put in to helping those people, the pre-schools and the after-school care that she has set up is just astounding.

You had the opportunity to listen to people like Salome yesterday with the African Women's Network. A woman that has only been in Ireland twelve years but by golly has she made a difference. Or people like Timmy Adbari, who lives in Portlaoise, and the work he has done in Ireland for the past six years. He has a Ph.D. in culturism from, I think, DCU. He has been involved in the whole area of inter-culturism and has started his own radio station, as well as being involved in politics. Two hundred yards down the road here, in The Brothers of Charity Service, there are people in the community here, working with people with disabilities, involving them in life, engaging them, asking them, giving them choices about their lives. They are not providing a service for them, they are providing a service with them. But yet we see so many situations where the services that we provide are *for* people rather than *with* them.

I return to the first question I posed in asking again, how do we fill our days? What do we do in terms of empowering and engaging people rather than just doing things for people? 'Give a man a fish and you feed him for a day, teach him how to fish and you feed him for life.' How we fill our day is an important thing. I know Mary Kealy is here, the Director of that service [The Brothers of Charity, Clare]. The same thing is happening in Roscommon and if they are good news stories and they are making a huge difference in the lives of people with a disability then why don't we know more about them? It is all about involving people, giving them a life, allowing them to be part and parcel of the communities we live in. Everybody has the right to be part of the community in which they live.

So those are just examples of people with powerful ideas and visions for confronting problems. There are many other stories right across a broad spectrum of issues and problems, stories of people making a positive change, bringing fresh thinking, new ideas, new solutions to some of the most entrenched social problems that we have. I believe we need to look out the highest-storey window of that virtual hotel at the top of Mount Everest and tell people what we are doing, how we are doing it and how we can replicate it right across the island to make a real difference in peoples' lives.

I was genuinely inspired by the students who are reporting here. I think they talked so much common sense. We sometimes speak of our young as being the future, but we could see here today that they are not just the future, they are the present too. They are not citizens in waiting, they are citizens, they are participating and they are making a huge difference. I do believe they will continue to make a huge difference if they are encouraged, if they are supported and if they are applauded for the work they do and the way in which they do it. We need to try to turn some of what we perceive as the negatives into positives, for example, the drinking they described at home rather than out in the pubs. Is there a way that we can use this experience as family members? I have four children between the ages of seventeen and twenty-four so I know exactly what goes on and I know about the drinking in the house before they go out. But I really do try to make an effort if I can with them to go into the kitchen or whatever room they have chosen that is free in the house and actually just chat to them, get to know their friends, what they are up to, what they are doing. All sorts of things have resulted out of doing that. In relation to just one issue, youth voting and registration, an issue for me on the Taskforce, I succeeded in getting the majority of my daughter's friends interested in registration and voting just by chatting with them. As we know, one in four between the ages of eighteen and twenty-four are not even registered to vote, let alone voting. So sometimes they just need to be made aware, they need somebody to support them, they need somebody to talk to them. And we always say and we know it, '*mol an oige agus tiocfaidh siad*' [praise the youth and they will come] and I think it is important and I think it is something that we should keep to the forefront of our minds.

About a year ago I was asked to talk to students in Trinity College about active citizenship, volunteering and engaging. I was absolutely delighted to be invited back there again a couple of weeks ago. Arising out of the talk that we did nearly a year ago, they had now set up a volunteer forum and they had all sorts of different activities going on in the universities. When you see universities and all those students involved you know there are great things going on. I agree with everything John Quinn said about education and I had that in my speech to talk about. It is a bit of a rat race; there are no incentives for young people to become involved in extra curricular activities because the points system is so, so strong. We need to enable and facilitate learning because as long as it is structured in the way that it is it will continue to be points driven and there won't be accreditation for participation like we see in some of the third levels.

But who can change that, with whom does the power lie? As one of the students said, they are more than the number of TDs in the Dáil. We all have the power. There are over four million of us and we have the power. It was Mahatma Gandhi that said 'be the change you want to see in the world'. We have got to take that responsibility and figure out ourselves where exactly the democracy lies. And if I have any power at all on the Taskforce, together with Harry and Catherine Eddery, who is also here, and my other colleagues, it will certainly be to make some recommendation around that whole area of education. I am not just talking about that formal education because I think it was John that said this morning that 20 per cent of our time is spent with formal education. But what happens the informal? Linking the formal and the non-formal is so critical, getting that SOS [Sharing our Skills] that John talked about earlier. We need to use the talent, the wisdom, the experience and the time of older people and use the knowledge and the dynamism that we saw this afternoon and the vibrancy and the quick mentality that youngsters have as well. We have got to use both of those. We have got to knit them together, I believe, and then we will get one heck of a *báinín* jumper that Ireland can wear with pride.

I said I would go back to the challenges and the big challenge that we have is how to stop the pressures that come as an unwanted appendix to this modern lifestyle that we have created for ourselves. We can look at what is there already and decide how to use it or change it or adapt it. I think that is when the best things are done oftentimes, when we look, see something that it might be possible to adapt in some way and use it. When you consider the job situation, we have job sharing in Ireland, we have flexi time and we have leave of absence. Is it being taken up, why is it not being taken up and if it is being taken up who is taking it up? Is it mainly women taking up flexi time, job sharing, leave of absence? It is not that men don't want to do it. I don't believe that is the case for one moment. I think men want to, fathers want to be at home with their children if they can, mothers want to be at home with their children if they can. So how can we make that possible? Can we ever arrive at a society in Ireland where it is possible, on a more equal basis, for both mother and father, man and woman, if they wish to do something else, to take that flexi time, to take that time out, but not be penalised for doing so? That is one of the fears, I believe, with men at the moment. They are afraid and they are perceived still in some ways as the breadwinners and women are perceived as the carers, though both these perceptions are changing. But can we ever get to a society where you will still get promotion and you won't be cut because you have the desire and you want to avail of what is there? I think we need to get towards a society in total acceptance of this. If careers weren't threatened, I believe people would avail of all the options. I believe society would change as a result of it. I believe we would have more time to spend with our children. They may not need all the gadgets or the €100 boots that we provide because of absence and guilt. We can cook, perhaps, rather than spend double the amount of money on the convenience food and the convenience stores that other speakers told of earlier on. I think we need to look at ways in which we can actually make the home the focal point and I think that if we do that the community part will follow as well.

In finishing, I will go back to one of the wonderful quotes John used earlier on today. 'Let go, let fly, forget, forget, you have listened long enough, now strike your note', and that is what I would like to challenge you all to do.

Filling the Vacuum?

The Céifin Centre for Values-Led Change is about holding a mirror up to the reality of modern society. Based in Shannon, it has been doing this in different ways since its foundation in 1998. One of these ways is through its annual conference, which now attracts over 500 people from a cross-section of Irish society and is the focus of widespread media coverage.

Despite our increasing prosperity, there is a growing sense of isolation and disconnectedness in Irish society. For that reason the theme 'filling the vacuum' was chosen for Conference 2005. What interventions are needed to establish and promote a strong sense of belonging within our society? This was a particularly successful conference, very well attended, with excellent presentations and lively feedback from the floor. These presentations are now contained in this publication and make compelling reading for those of us working towards a better society.

filling the vacuum?

Contributors
Rachael English • Mary McAleese • Eoin O'Driscoll • Marie Murray
Pat Duffy • Peter McVerry • Denis Bradley • Mary Surlis
Telling My Story
Cian Ó Síocháin • Alan Kerins • Jean Butler • Caroline Casey

EDITED BY HARRY BOHAN

978 1 85390 947 4
€12.95

Imagining the Future

Ireland as a society is in a unique position at this moment in time. Over the last ten years our standard of living has increased, while at the same time our belief in state and religious institutions has dwindled. However, the issue of how to relate to one another and to the wider world is only beginning to be explored, as is the issue of becoming a multi-cultural society.

Contributors include Archbishop Diarmuid Martin, Emily O'Reilly (Ireland's Ombudsman), Michael D. Higgins, Catherine Byrne (the Deputy General Secretary of the Irish National Teachers' Organisation), Mike Cooley (Chairman of the Joint EU/India Scientific Committee and a chief consultant to the UN on technological impacts) and Tina Roche (Chief Executive of The Foundation for Investing in Communities).

978 1 85390 804 0

€12.95

Global Aspirations and the Reality of Change

How can we do things differently?

Just imagine experiencing a feast of stories, ideas, dialogue, music, drama and good conversation …

Just imagine being transported through the revolution that Ireland has experienced in the past decade – the rise and rise in consumption, the acceleration in the pace of work and personal life, the effect of communication replacing transmission, the means overcoming the end … but despite all that, imagine that change is possible. Imagine a revolution of deceleration.

'Indifference will not be allowed': imagine the challenge of these five words!

Just imagine having a whole morning to reflect on the possibilities of influencing the system of power that keeps us politically docile and economically productive. Imagine the joy of realising that power is present in every moment, in every relationship and there is ultimately no 'small act'.

Just imagine all that and the camaraderie and the energy of spending two days with three hundred people who want to do things differently, who want to effect change. Imagine conversations – at early and late hours – stories, dreams, ideas, debate, energy.

978 1 85390 742 5 • €13.95

Values and Ethics

can I make a difference?

What are the values that we choose to prioritise and live by? What price are we prepared to pay for ethics? Is it enough to rely on the law as the minimum standard of acceptable behaviour? Ultimately, can one person make a difference?

These and other far-reaching questions are addressed in *Values and Ethics,* the fifth collection of papers from the Céifin conference which is held annually in Ennis, Co. Clare. Contributors include Professor Robert Putnam (author of *Bowling Alone*), sociologist Dr Tony Fahey, Bishop Willie Walsh and Dr Lorna Gold from the University of York.

There is a belief in Ireland that we have not adjusted to our new-found prosperity. In a society that measures almost everything in monetary terms, values and ethics are increasingly sidelined. We now face the challenge of taking our social growth as seriously as we take our economic growth.

This book gives hope that real change can begin with committed individuals who believe passionately that shared values can become a social reality.

978 1 85390 658 9 • €13.95

Is The Future My Responsibility?

Have we become helpless in the face of change or can we manage the future? More and more people talk about the emptiness of modern life; they wonder where meaning is coming from and what values are shaping us; they say it is not easy being young today in spite of the choices and the freedom. We cannot assume that if we simply sit back and comment the storm will blow over, or that we will return to the old ways. The fact is we are experiencing a cultural transformation, we are witnessing the passing of a tradition, the end of an era. Every day we hear questions like 'Why aren't they doing something about it?' or 'Who is responsible for this, that or the other?' It is time to ask: 'Have I got any responsibility for the way things are?'

Including contributions from Nobel Laureate John Hume and internationally renowned writer and broadcaster Charles Handy, *Is the Future My Responsibility?* is the fourth book of papers from the Céifin conference, held annually in Ennis, County Clare, and published by Veritas.

978 1 85390 605 3 • €12.50